BY PHILLIP J. WINGATE

Before the Bridge

The Beasts of Big Business

The Colorful DuPont Company

H. L. Mencken's Un-Neglected Anniversary

Bandages of Soft Illusion

Before the Bridge

Before the Bridge

Reminiscences by

PHILLIP J. WINGATE, 1913-

Tidewater Publishers : Centreville, Maryland

Grateful acknowledgment is made to Alfred A. Knopf, Inc. for
permission to quote from the copyrighted works of H. L. Mencken.

Library of Congress Cataloging in Publication Data

Wingate, P. J. (Phillip Jerome), 1913-
    Before the bridge.

    1. Wingate, P. J. (Phillip Jerome), 1913-
2. Dorchester County (Md.)—Biography.   3. Chesapeake Bay
Region (Md. and Va.)—Biography.   4. Dorchester County
(Md.)—Social life and customs.   5. Chesapeake Bay Region
(Md. and Va.)—Social life and customs.   I. Title.
F187.D6W57 1985   975.2'2704'0924   84-26694
ISBN 0-87033-329-1

Manufactured in the United States of America

First edition

To all the Wingates who tried to mold, shape,
and improve me during my twenty-nine years
along the shores of the Chesapeake Bay,
and to Sue Smith Wingate who has had the same assignment
for the forty-two years since I moved away from the Bay.
They all had, at best, only moderate success.

Contents

List of Illustrations

xi

Preface

THE sunrise years of my life were spent in various locations along the Chesapeake Bay. During that time I was exposed to a wide variety of things such as mosquitoes, muskrats, marked playing cards, opera stars, corn borers, Epsom salts, lacrosse, H. L. Mencken, Curley Byrd, and finally the chemical structure of sex hormones and insecticides.

It was all very interesting—even fascinating at times—and when I left the shores of the Chesapeake, the sun was well above the horizon and shining brightly.

Before the Bridge

Dorchester

DORCHESTER County is a peninsula lying between the two largest rivers on the Eastern Shore of Maryland, the Nanticoke on the east and the Choptank on the west and north. It is the largest county on the Shore including 688 square miles, according to the mapmakers, and almost was an island. In fact, if the Marshyhope Creek which branches off the Nanticoke River north of Vienna had continued west for another five miles, instead of turning north, it would have run into the Choptank, causing all but a tiny bit of Dorchester to be surrounded by salt water from the Chesapeake.

Aubrey Bodine, the *Baltimore Sun*'s famous artist with a camera who photographed every section of Maryland, said that Dorchester was easily the most scenic county in the state, and he had many good reasons for making this statement.

Dorchester is a land of rivers, marshes, and pine trees which catch the eye of any artist who sees them. The marshes are particularly beautiful but so are the rivers.

In addition to the broad Choptank and Nanticoke rivers which bound Dorchester on two sides, there are the Little Choptank, the Honga, the Transquaking, the Chicamacomico, and the Blackwater which is perhaps the most scenic of them all. Its still, dark waters reflecting the low marsh grasses along its banks, the clumps of taller phragmites and cattails, and lonely stands of loblolly pines, are enchantingly beautiful.

In addition to its many rivers, Dorchester has Fishing Bay entirely within its boundaries, while Tangier Sound and Hooper Strait lie partly within the county and surround Bloodsworth and Holland islands at the southern tip of it all.

Before the Bridge

A good way to visualize what Dorchester County looks like from the air is to turn your right hand palm up and place it flat on a table in front of you. The Nanticoke River then lies just left of the little finger while the Choptank lies above the thumb. The Little Choptank separates the thumb from the index finger, and the neck district, with its own four creeks and many necks of land, sticking out north and south, is represented by the thumb. Cambridge, which looks out across the broad water of the Choptank, is located at the point where the thumb is attached to the rest of the hand.

Taylors Island and Cattail Island then run into Hooper Island, represented by the index finger, which is separated from the two middle fingers by the Honga River. Fishing Bay separates the little finger from these two middle fingers which together point down to Bloodsworth and Holland islands, the southern tip of Dorchester.

My father built his house near the tip of the small peninsula represented by those two middle fingers. From our house I could look west across Fox Creek and the Honga River to Hooper Island or south toward Crab Point and Hooper Strait. To the east was Toddville and directly east of it was Fishing Bay and Elliott Island.

Except where there is water, there are marshes in all directions because most of the southern half of Dorchester is only a foot or two above sea level. There are ridges and isolated areas of higher ground which are five to ten feet above sea level but these are exceptional areas. One of the ridges, or spines, ran through the middle of my father's farm and another one lay two miles toward the east and provided high ground for most of the homes in Toddville and Bishops Head. Elliott Island and Asquith Island are examples of the isolated areas of high ground. Neither one is a true island but simply an area of somewhat higher ground surrounded by water on three sides and marshland on the fourth. Both Elliott and Asquith islands were highly fertile and grew excellent crops of vegetables, fruits, and grains during my sixteen years in Dorchester.

I learned things from the fields, forests, and waters of Dorchester, but the marshes taught me more than the other

4

Dorchester

three. This was partly because the marshes covered so much of the land area around me, but it was mostly, I believe, because these marshes were teeming with animal life of many kinds, and I had close at hand a gifted naturalist who found it amusing to discuss the subject with my brothers and me. This gifted naturalist was our family physician, Dr. Patrick Henry Tawes, and his views on the ecology of south Dorchester were startling then. Such views have all become well accepted in recent decades.

The fleshy part of the thumb and an inch or so of the wrist, in our hand map of Dorchester, include Hurlock, East New Market, and most of the agricultural area of the county. This area has its own points of interest, but they do not make Dorchester stand out from Kent and Talbot counties or even Frederick and Carroll on the western shore.

The marshes are what make Dorchester a unique part of Maryland, and the heartland of these marshes lay about ten miles north of where my father had made his home. This is the area which includes the Transquaking, Chicamacomico, and Blackwater rivers, and is the location for the now famous Blackwater National Wildlife Refuge. The area stretches only about twenty miles from east to west and slightly less from north to south, and so it might seem that the three rivers which run through the area should be counted as mere creeks in the marsh. However, the situation is deceptive because these rivers take so many twists and turns that they are several times as long as they appear to be on a map. The Blackwater, in particular, since it has three branches, probably has a total length of fifty or sixty miles. It is all very close to sea level and so is in no hurry to get anywhere. It rambles around through the marshes in such a manner that a raindrop falling in the Blackwater west of Route 335 may take a week or two before it finally flows into Fishing Bay. The salt water from Fishing Bay has an even more difficult time working its way along the bottom of the river toward the heart of the wildlife refuge. All of which, no doubt, please the muskrats, ducks, geese, and other forms of wildlife which abound there.

Certainly, the great marshy area around these three small

rivers is ideally suited to one form of animal life—the mosquito. As Dr. Tawes once said to me, "If there ever was a Garden of Eden for mosquitoes it was in and around the Blackwater River." Dr. Tawes had a name for mosquitoes, which he professed to admire; he called them "the protectors."

The Protectors

MY mother and father had eight children. The first of these, a boy named Reginald, died when he was about one year old, but my parents managed to raise the other seven to maturity, no simple feat back in the days before the discovery of sulfa drugs, penicillin, and polio vaccine.

The first four of the seven survivors were boy, girl, boy, girl, but the last three were all boys. I was the middle one in that final three and by the mid-1920s only Vic, Mark, and I were living at home. The others were all working away or going to college. Thus it was that my mother was running a boys' camp in an area almost ideally suited for such a project.

We had water, fields, forests, and marshes all around us, and wildlife was abundant in all these places—particularly in the marshes. It probably was inevitable, under those circumstances, that I would become a naturalist of a sort, and the kind I became was greatly influenced by three men: my father, Dr. Patrick Henry Tawes, our family physician, and Ernest Thompson Seton, a British naturalist and writer.

Seton started life as Ernest Seton Thompson but for reasons of his own reversed his last two names when he became a writer. When my two brothers and I were still in grammar school, my father bought us a set of books by Mr. Thompson-Seton and they delighted us. Included among them were *Two Little Savages* and *Wild Animals I Have Known*. There were several others including *The Biography of a Grizzly*, but the first two were our favorites.

Seton spent many years in Canada, and *Two Little Savages* was the story of two white boys, about our age, living on a farm in Canada but trying to imitate the Indians. It was a fascinating

7

story and after we read it, my brothers and I spent the next two years making bows and arrows and wigwams thatched with pine straw. We also spent many hours trying to start a fire by rubbing two sticks together or by using an advanced fire-making technique, described in detail by Seton, which involved spinning a wooden stick in a notched board so that the frictional heat would be increased, thereby causing the wood to burst into flame. Our devices never did burst into flame although we often produced smoke and a few glowing coals.

While *Two Little Savages* was my favorite book I suspect that *Wild Animals I Have Known* did more to educate me. Seton held the point of view, not common then but rather widespread now, that animals are as much entitled to a place in the world as people are. In fact, I got the impression that he may have believed that animals, in general, were better behaved than people and therefore more deserving of a place in the scheme of things. My father occasionally expressed similar opinions and Dr. Tawes often did.

Of all the stories about animals Seton had known, my favorite was the one about Wully, a "yaller dog" who served as assistant to a sheepherder, named Robin, in Scotland. A yaller dog, Seton explained, was quite different from a yellow dog. The latter could be a pedigreed canine while a yaller dog was always a mongrel with a lot more intelligence than his elite counterpart. Wully was exceptionally intelligent even for a yaller dog. He had been trained by an older sheep dog and by Old Robin, the hard drinking sheepherder who was, according to Seton, not much inferior in intelligence to the two dogs who assisted him. Wully was loyal to his stupid master, beyond the point of good sense, but finally became separated from him when Robin sent Wully on a senseless search for a sheep, which was not really missing, and then abandoned him. Wully searched for this worthless god of his for weeks but finally gave up and found a new master. Everything went well then for a while until Wully, perhaps frustrated by memories of his previous master or maybe just responding to his inherent nature, turned sheep killer instead of sheepherder and had to be destroyed. His death saddened my brothers and me greatly.

Cornelia McNamara Wingate and Charles Millard Mead Wingate. While the mosquitoes were the "protectors" of the great marshes of Dorchester County, Charles and Cornelia Wingate were the protectors of the Wingate children who grew up in these same marshes.

Before the Bridge

We had a yaller dog ourselves. She was named Trixie, and she was just as intelligent and loyal as Wully had been before he becamed disillusioned. My father trained her to do many tricks, one of which must have been extremely difficult for her. He had her take a note, wrapped around a penny, to the grocery store a quarter of a mile away. The note instructed the storekeeper to give Trixie one ginger cookie—in her mouth—and send her back home. She always arrived with the cookie thoroughly wet with saliva but otherwise undamaged until my father said: "Eat." Then it disappeared in one quick gulp.

Trixie was a natural herder and without training of any kind that I remember she learned how to herd a flock of geese which my mother maintained for several years. She never hurt one of them even when they were tiny goslings.

One day I was walking with Trixie in our lower field when she spotted the only baby killdeer I ever saw. The killdeer nests were plentiful in our fields and I saw hundreds of their eggs, but as baby birds their camouflage was so good that I never saw, before that day, a killdeer too young to fly. This one was still slightly moist and made no attempt to run away even though its mother was making frantic efforts to distract Trixie and me, feigning both a broken leg and two broken wings. Trixie looked at the baby bird for a second or two, then trotted ahead a few paces and looked back at me, obviously encouraging me to follow her and leave the young bird alone.

When I told my father about this thoughtful behavior, he said: "It doesn't surprise me. I have always thought that Trixie has more sense than most of the people I know."

Trixie remained loyal to the end to her first and only family of humans, and so far as I know never had any hidden longings to revert to savagery.

Mr. Seton wrote about all his wild animal friends with the same sympathetic understanding which he had for Wully. He gave them individual personalities and wrote with compassion for their yearnings and cravings. He explained his attitude by noting, in one of his books, that any account of the human race which covered only its general behavior and characteristics would surely be dull or even repulsive, while accounts of individual human beings often show them to be interesting and attractive creatures.

Grizzly bears and wolves were favorite animals of Seton, and he was not bothered by what other people regarded as their savage behavior. They killed to eat, he said, much like people killed rabbits, chickens, and hogs, and therefore wild animals should not be counted as evil because they killed. The only animal that he did not invest with a nobility of some sort was the groundhog, which played an important role in *Two Little Savages*. However, this story was about boys and was written from their perspective rather than from the point of view of the groundhog.

There were no wolves and grizzly bears in south Dorchester and for that matter no groundhogs either. If the wolves and grizzlies had ever roamed there, they had moved on to more hospitable territory after the white man took over, but the groundhog almost certainly never lived there. This can be said with some certainty because the groundhog hibernates during the winter, digging himself a hole below the frost line and staying there until spring, or at least until February 2 when he is supposed to come out briefly and predict the weather for the next month or so. If any ground hog in ancient times had been tempted by the lush vegetation of summer to move into south Dorchester, he would have surely found out when winter came that any hole he dug quickly filled with water. Not only was all land in our community close to sea level and salt water, but underground water was also close to the surface.

However, while we had no groundhogs, other forms of wildlife were abundant. The woods had a plentiful supply of rabbits, raccoons, opossums, foxes, and squirrels. My brothers and I caught all of these animals, except squirrels, in our rabbit traps.

A south Dorchester rabbit trap was a simple device, consisting of four boards, about a foot wide and four feet long, nailed together to make a tunnel which was permanently closed at one end but which had a trapdoor at the other end. A notched stick inside the tunnel, near the closed end, activated the trapdoor when a rabbit tried to eat the bait which was placed there. Rabbits were lured inside the tunnel by a piece of onion placed near the notched stick which activated the trapdoor. Rabbits are vegetarians and the odor of a fresh onion probably was as appealing to them as hot onion soup is to people.

We ate the rabbits which we trapped, and when I asked my father about this one time, he reminded me that we had to eat and so should not worry about eating rabbits. It reminded me of Mr. Seton and his wolves and grizzlies and I let it go at that, but I suspect my father did not enjoy his assignment which was to kill our rabbits by striking them on the back of their necks. He never allowed any hunting in his woods or fields and he never went goose or duck hunting, but he enjoyed roast duck or goose as much as the rest of us did.

Although red foxes were plentiful around Fox Creek and occasionally came out of the woods to steal chickens, we caught only one fox in our rabbit traps. Foxes are meat eaters and so the onion probably did not lure him into the trap. Since he was a young fox, he was probably just nosing around trying to find out something about the world around him. We named him Uncas and kept him as a pet for several weeks, feeding him chicken parts and other table scraps, until he escaped one night by digging a hole under the chicken wire which we had used to make a pen for him.

We caught more rabbits than anything else in our traps, but we also caught a lot of opossums, which everyone in south Dorchester called by the shortened name of possum. These gray, long-furred little animals with the long hairless tails had personalities as interesting as any of the animals described by Seton. What intrigued my brothers and me most about them was their habit of grinning and playing possum.

A possum could be dumped out of a trap onto the ground but instead of running away he would be perfectly still, apparently dead. But if everyone went away or hid behind a tree, in a few minutes the possum would come to life and amble off in that slow waddling gait which was characteristic of possums. They usually traveled only by night but occasionally were seen during the day. If a dog came upon him, the possum would play dead just as he did with people. Whether this defense mechanism worked against foxes as well as it did with less sophisticated animals, such as boys and dogs, I do not know, but it must have been generally effective since possums were plentiful in south Dorchester.

However, if a fox was too smart to be fooled by an apparently dead possum, the possum had another defense—a row of menacing looking teeth which he probably used in any desperate situation. There is an old saying in many southern states which goes: "he was grinning like a possum caught sucking eggs." This grinning act of a possum was, of course, a snarl, a pulling back of the lips to show that row of sharp teeth. But the fascinating thing about a possum's snarl is that it really does look like a grin.

No one ate possums in our community in those days, even though roast possum has long been famous as a delicacy in Virginia, Georgia, Alabama, and other states of the deep South. So we made pets of our captured possums. They invariably escaped after a few weeks, digging out under the chicken wire, as Uncas had done, or finding some other escape route, but while they were around we petted them and stroked their backs like so many pussycats. They often grinned at us but never took a bite out of our hands, or even tried to.

Consequently, it always pleases me today when I encounter evidence that the possum is still a thriving species. Not only are they abundant in Dorchester County but all over Maryland and Delaware. The possum does not live just in the woods anymore; they thrive in suburbia and even in fairly large cities where they have learned how to find food in various urban spots such as garbage cans. My daughter, Barbara, recently told me she had seen a strange looking, furry little animal waiting to cross the street one night only a few blocks from the center of Wilmington, Delaware. It was being trailed by four smaller animals of the same sort and when the large animal reached the curb, it stopped and the four small ones climbed on its back but later dismounted on the other side of the street. It was, of course, a mother possum and her four babies, all of them proving just how adaptable the possum really is. The future might seem secure to any wild animal which knows how to cross streets.

However, while the possum has learned to handle slow moving city traffic, it has not yet learned how to cope with fast moving cars on country highways. Every spring and fall dozens of them can be seen smashed on the roads. Apparently the possum tries its old trick of playing dead when it thinks it is in imminent danger and so it stops in the middle of the road, and in a second or two it really is dead. But any animal which can fool city dogs and country boys, and has a snarl so benign in appearance that it looks like a grin will surely learn how to handle even fast cars in a few generations. Vive la possum!

We had an enormous variety of birds in south Dorchester during the 1920s—everything from eagles and buzzards to wrens and hummingbirds. Other sections of Maryland had many of our birds also—the robins, mockingbirds, cardinals, blue jays, larks, blackbirds, sparrows, and many others—but those other areas, fifty or a hundred feet above sea level or even higher, lacked our marsh birds—the bitterns, killdeers, rail-birds, geese, ducks, swans, seagulls, ospreys, eagles, and loons.

The marshes also harbored a host of other forms of animal life. Snapping turtles and muskrats were abundant, and the periwinkles, or marsh snails, could be counted in the billions. There must have been several million of these creatures in the narrow strip of marsh which lay between Fox Creek and the road which ran in front of our house. They ranged in size from baby snails no bigger than a grain of salt up to grand-fathers as big as the end of a man's thumb. It fascinated me to watch them move up and down on the marsh grass as the tide rose and fell. My father said they ate microorganisms which they found on the blades of marsh grass they were clinging to, and in turn were eaten by the railbirds or marsh hens as we called them. There were not many muskrats in the marshes near our house because the water in these marshes was too salty to grow the three-square grass which muskrats love to eat. There was one family of muskrats near the northwest corner

The Protectors

of our property, and my father often threatened to set a trap and catch them, but he never did it. The area around the Blackwater River, ten miles north of us, was ideally suited to them, and the muskrat population there probably ran as high as several hundred thousand.

The waters of south Dorchester were also teeming with life. During the summer blue crabs swam in every creek and ditch which crisscrossed the marshes and drained into Fishing Bay and Honga River. These voracious creatures ate everything, alive or dead, which had protein in it if they could get their claws on it. My brothers and I grew ducks for several years. We never ate them but did ship some to Baltimore for sale from time to time. However, while they were with us we treated them as pets and even had names for each duck. Every year after a new batch of yellow baby ducks hatched, we noticed that when the mother duck took them out into the nearest branch of Fox Creek, she sometimes came back with one or two less ducks than she went out with. It puzzled me that the mother duck could be so careless with her children until I happened to be watching them one day and saw a crab swim up, seize a baby by its webbed foot, and drag it under the surface. I dashed into the water and saved this duckling, but after that I knew where the others had gone.

A half mile from my father's house, when the tide was low, oysters could be picked up on the mud flats of Fox Creek, and snouted clams, which we called mananose, could be dug from the somewhat sandy mud nearer the shore. Steamed, the mananose was one of the great delicacies of south Dorchester, but the oysters from Fox Creek were not very good. They usually had a muddy taste and were not as salty or tasty as oysters from the area where Fishing Bay and the Nanticoke River flowed into Tangier Sound. But the blue crabs, no matter where they came from, were always delicious when steamed, and it apparently didn't make any difference whether they had baby duckling for breakfast or not. The baked shad and broiled rockfish were also always delicious no matter what body of water they came from.

It might seem, at first glance, that with two brothers close enough in age to be suitable companions and a superabundance of wildlife to look at that I had an idyllic boyhood. Alas, that was not the case. For the most part, to be sure, the lines did fall unto me in pleasant places, as the psalmist says, and I would not pick another location to grow up in if I could, but not everything was pleasant.

For example, there were the mosquitoes. If we had billions of periwinkles near us, there were trillions of mosquitoes—perhaps even quadrillions or quintillions of them.

I can't remember when I was first bitten by a mosquito but it probably was when I was about five months old. I was born in January and mosquitoes did not make their presence felt until about June, but by July there simply was no way to avoid them. They were incredibly ingenious and determined. No screen we ever tried could turn back all of them. If the big ones could not get through, their younger brothers and their biting sisters did. And no alleged chemical deterrent, either gaseous or liquid, could cause them to desert the field of battle.

There were two tactics which my parents and their neighbors used in trying to keep the mosquitoes under control during the peak of their season. One was to build a smudge fire, using rags or leaves, and hope the smoke would drive the mosquitoes away. It never did, although the smoke got so objectionable at times that it drove the people away. Whereupon the mosquitoes followed them. The other technique was to rub oil of citronella on all exposed surfaces of the body, but this was just as ineffective as the smoke. I have seen a dozen or two mosquitoes busily pumping blood from an arm which had just been lavishly anointed with oil of citronella. These futile attempts to keep the mosquitoes from biting us continued year after year in south Dorchester, perhaps because a few timid ones really were driven away but mostly, I believe, because a person in a desperate situation wants to do something whether it works or not.

No one I ever knew was totally immune to the pain caused by a mosquito bite, but all of us who lived in south Dorchester did develop a sort of immunity to the swelling which was produced in strangers who visited in the mosquito season.

The Protectors

When my oldest brother, Wilson, brought his new wife home for a visit one September, she quickly developed fifty or a hundred welts on her arms and legs, much like the lumps caused by a bee sting. She was a native of St. Mary's County and had been bitten by mosquitoes before but these earlier bites never caused her to grow welts like those produced by what she called our "flying rattlesnakes."

It probably was this swelling which resulted when our mosquitoes bit strangers which caused the often repeated rumors that Dorchester mosquitoes were the largest in the world. There was no truth to these claims. We had mosquitoes of all sizes, of course, but the adults were no bigger than mosquitoes in Maine, Alaska, or New Jersey, for example. However, the virulence of the fluid which they injected to hasten the flow of blood in their victims may have been unique. I think it was. And when a visitor returned home and was trying to explain the lumps on his face and arms, he probably felt compelled to give an explanation which he thought his listeners would believe. So he said he had been bitten by mosquitoes as big as horseflies, hummingbirds, or hawks. It all depended on how imaginative he was to start with. But it *was* all imagination. Our mosquitoes certainly were not unique in size, but they may have been in venom, and they surely were in number. I have seen them arise from a tomato field or a marsh, when someone walked by and disturbed them, in swarms which literally darkened the air a few feet above ground.

But whatever the facts were about size, venom, and numbers, Dorchester mosquitoes did have a reputation for ferocity, and I believe it was deserved. When visitors to our community stopped by the post office, where my father worked, or the bank, where Mr. Murphy was cashier, they always complained about the mosquitoes if it was summertime. And if Dr. Patrick Tawes happened to be there when the complaint was made, the visitor always received a surprising lecture. Dr. Tawes professed to admire mosquitoes, and he ascribed to them a personality much in the way that Ernest Thompson-Seton personalized the animals he wrote about.

Before the Bridge

Dr. Tawes was the only physician in south Dorchester, and I suspect that he was a somewhat lonely man, wthout many close personal friends in the community except my father and Mr. Murphy. He usually stopped by the bank or post office each day so that he, Mr. Murphy, and my father could swap stories. As the only doctor in south Dorchester, he surely was exposed to so much sadness, grief, and death that he probably needed these stories to offset the tragedy. Perhaps all three of these friends needed some humor to help them along. Anyway, they regularly told each other humorous stories, and if no new ones were available, they dipped into their inventories and repeated old ones. They generally paid no attention if boys were present, and I heard Dr. Tawes on the subject of mosquitoes many times. The essence of what he had to say was that the mosquito was the noblest form of animal life because it had more courage than any other living creature.

"The mosquito," Dr. Tawes said, "should replace the eagle as our national bird because it is much braver. I have seen an eagle driven from its nest in the marshes near Crisfield by a ten-year-old boy but a mosquito will, without hesitation, attack a man weighing about a million times as much. He will even attack a full grown bull weighing ten million times as much and he doesn't sneak up and try to bite the bull in some hidden spot the way a flea or a tick does. He will bite him right on the end of his nose. A man with comparable courage would have to charge a herd of elephants armed only with a hatpin."

When Dr. Tawes gave these lectures in praise of mosquitoes, my father kept a deadpan expression that revealed nothing. But Mr. Murphy would turn his back, and I could see his shoulders shake and the tips of his handlebar mustache tremble. Dr. Tawes had several variations of his mosquito story, and one of them said the mosquito had been created by the Lord to help bring some measure of courage to the human race.

"A man is almost always a pusillanimous coward," he said, "and the Lord has probably been ashamed of this disgraceful lack of courage ever since He created the human race. So He designed the mosquito with two purposes in mind. One was to

The Protectors

have the mosquito draw out some of a man's cowardly blood and the other was to replace it with an injection of courage. That is why a mosquito bite is a painful thing. Courage has a lot of sting in it."

Most of the visitors who heard Dr. Tawes looked at him in stunned silence but on rare occasions one talked back. This happened one day when I was present while he delivered his piece about the injection of courage.

"You people down here," the man said, "must be the bravest people on earth by now or else you were the damndest cowards that ever lived before the mosquitoes started working on you."

When I was in my second year of high school our biology teacher, Miss Andrews, introduced us to what she called the "food chain." She said that all those delicious protein dishes which we had in Dorchester—oysters, crabs, shad, black ducks, etc.—started with microscopic forms of life in the marshes and worked their way up the scale, getting tastier each step of the way. This microscopic marsh life fed the mosquitoes in their larval or wriggler stage, and the wriggler mosquitoes were eaten by baby fish, tadpoles, and similar things. These, in turn, were eaten by crabs, ducks, diamondback terrapins, shad fish, and other high ranking forms of protein. She built up an entire pyramid, starting with mosquitoes on the bottom and ending with people on the top. It was the first time I had ever heard anyone offer a serious justification for the existence of mosquitoes. Since I thought Dr. Tawes would like it, I told him about the food chain Miss Andrews had diagrammed. He looked briefly at this diagram I had brought along and said Miss Andrews had turned it upside down.

"The mosquito should be right at the top, just above the human race, because the mosquito is the only wild animal which regularly feeds on people. A shark or a tiger may eat a man every now and then, but they always kill him while the mosquito looks upon the human race much the same way people look upon a herd of cows. The mosquito draws off some blood, as it is needed, just as we milk cows, but he has no desire to kill the beast which feeds him. In fact, the mosquito is probably the best behaved man-eating animal in the world. He takes what he needs and no more."

I told Dr. Tawes that Miss Andrews explained that only female mosquitoes bit, but he quickly said that was wrong.

"Tell Miss Andrews to check her facts. Females just don't have the kind of courage which mosquitoes display every day. They are protectors and patriots who defend their territory with more courage than most men ever show."

I realized even then that Dr. Tawes had his tongue in his cheek when he sang the praises of mosquitoes, and I now suspect he knew Miss Andrews was right about only females biting but he stuck by his guns when I told him she said her facts were solid.

"It can't be so; there hasn't been a female with that kind of brazen courage since Queen Elizabeth sent Sir Francis Drake out to do piracy on the high seas. And even the Queen had a man to do her rough work."

Besides using his mosquito lectures to let off steam and provide some relief from his steady diet of disease and sorrow, I also suspect Dr. Tawes wanted me to understand that the world is a complicated place. No one has all the answers, there are always several ways to look at anything, and the funny way is often just as good as any other.

His reactions to swallows, blue tail flies, and blackberries were all cases in point. Swallows were abundant in south Dorchester. Their mud nests lined with fine straw could be found in most barns in the area and dozens of these nests were built each spring in the abandoned warehouse which stood on the edge of Fox Creek, about fifty yards from the post office. One reason why the swallows were so abundant was that they fed on mosquitoes and other small insects, eating them by the thousands as they went skimming over the marshes. One day our grammar school teacher, Miss Marguerite Kirwan, a dark-haired young beauty the same age as my oldest brother, told us that we should never disturb a swallow's nest.

"Swallows are our friends because they are enemies of the mosquito and eat millions of them."

This statement sounded reasonable to me but when I told

The Protectors

Dr. Tawes about it he promptly said Miss Marguerite was wrong.

"Swallows do eat a lot of mosquitoes, but that doesn't mean they are enemies. The swallow probably thinks that the mosquito is one of the great joys of this world, but he looks upon the human race as a menace or at best a damn nuisance. If the swallows had to choose either man or mosquitoes for extermination, I'm sure they would pick men. They eat mosquitoes but just enough to thin the herd and keep it healthy."

He also had a sympathetic reaction to blue tail flies, which were abundant during the summer because of a waste product from the crabbing industry. Most of the people in our community worked in the crabbing industry, either catching or preparing crabs for market. The soft shell crabs were no problem, but the hard shell crabs were. After they were steamed and most of the cooked meat had been picked from them, the residue was known as "crab bones." The farmers in south Dorchester had learned that crab bones were an excellent fertilizer because of their nitrogen and calcium content, and they regularly spread them on their tomato fields. This practice greatly increased the yield of tomatoes per acre but created two problems. A terrific stench was produced when the bits of remaining crab meat decayed, and the blue tail flies found the decomposing crab bones to be just what they wanted as a breeding ground. The result was that we had billions of blue tail flies coming out of the tomato fields every year.

The stench and the blue tails worried many people, even if not the farmers who were getting improved crops, and one summer our preacher, the Reverend Mr. Sutton, tried to get several of the nearby farmers to use a different fertilizer. They refused, and one of them said it obviously was the will of the Lord that crab bones be used on tomato fields or else the tomatoes would not grow so well under the treatment. I repeated this theory to Dr. Tawes one day because I thought he might have a different point of view, but as usual his reaction surprised me.

"He may be right. However, I always have more trouble than most people in trying to figure out what the will of the

Lord is. The crab bones do produce an awful lot of blue tail flies and these flies may spread a lot of disease, but on the other hand they certainly do increase the size of the tomato crop. And for all I know the Lord may be just as interested in having healthy tomato plants as in having healthy people. Maybe He is even interested in blue tail flies. When I was a boy in Sunday School, my teacher said the Lord knows about it when even one sparrow falls to the earth, and so perhaps He also looks out for blue tail flies."

Dr. Tawes's reaction to blackberries went beyond anything I had read in Mr. Seton's books. Blackberries grew wild in most places above the salt line in south Dorchester, and my brothers and I picked fifty to a hundred quarts each summer, for use at home and for sale in the community. Oddly enough, it seemed to me, the blackberry bushes were most plentiful in clearings in the pine woods several miles from where most of the people lived. One day Vic and I returned with about ten quarts and went over to the bank to offer some to Mr. Murphy because he was usually a good customer. Dr. Tawes was there, and he asked us where we had picked our berries.

"Up at Beechground," Vic replied, referring to an area about four miles from the bank and pretty far back in the woods.

"Did you ever stop to think why blackberries grow mostly in such out-of-the-way places?"

"No," Vic said, "we just go where they are."

"Well," replied Dr. Tawes, "they grow there because the blackberries have planned it that way. A blackberry bush, just like all other living things, would like to see more of its own kind growing in the world. That is why it grows berries with seeds in them, but if the seeds fall right under the bush and grow there, the patch soon becomes too crowded. So the bush makes its berries attractive to birds which eat them and drop the seeds at distant places. The birds build their nests in trees on the edges of clearings, and that is why you find the blackberry bushes there. The blackberry doesn't want to be eaten by people because people usually cook the berries first, and this kills the seeds. Even when people eat the berries uncooked, it

The Protectors

doesn't do the propagation of blackberries any good because people are disgustingly sanitary—at least from the point of view of the blackberry."

Then he turned toward Mr. Murphy and laughed before adding: "Of course the people in this community come closer to having sanitary habits which please the blackberry bushes than people in Cambridge or Baltimore do, but the blackberry still prefers birds to people."

Despite the beautiful scenery around the Blackwater and Transquaking rivers and the lower half of the Nanticoke, very few people live there today. The entire area is much like it was in 1608 when Captain John Smith explored and sailed up the Nanticoke. There may be more geese and fewer ducks, but the muskrat and mosquito populations are probably much the same as they were then when Captain John said the marshes were teeming with wildlife.

And I believe I know why this is so. Dr. Tawes put his finger on the answer when he called the mosquitoes the protectors and defenders of their territory. They have indeed defended their homeland with amazing success against the one species which might have drastically changed the area around the Blackwater and Nanticoke—people.

It is true that the upper half of the Nanticoke has changed. There are some villages and towns now, with a large power plant at Vienna and the first nylon plant in the world at Seaford, but the number of protectors along the Nanticoke from Vienna to Seaford is probably only a tenth of the number along the southern half of the river. And the mosquito is in complete control of the area around the Blackwater, Transquaking, and Chicamacomico rivers.

People have assailed the mosquito with just about every deadly device known to science, but still this tiny predator with the incomparable courage is in full control of his home territory. He has lost some battles but never a war.

Mosquitoes have drawn more of my blood than I ever wanted them to have, and I do not wish them well. But as Dr. Tawes would probably say, if he were still around, the mosquitoes surely don't give a damn how I feel about them.

THREE

Fourth of July at Crapo

WHEN I entered the first grade of school in 1919, World War I had ended less than a year earlier, and south Dorchester, like the rest of the country, was steeped in patriotism. This patriotic fervor manifested itself in three principal ways: hatred of Germany and Germans, love of our allies, particularly France and Belgium, and veneration of all things American.

My first school year was devoted to reading, writing, and arithmetic, and my twenty-year-old teacher, Miss Marguerite Kirwan, had no trouble with me on the first and third of these subjects but writing was another matter. Miss Marguerite's writing was a thing of beauty, fully equal to the copybooks we all worked from, and it remained that way for the next half a century. My handwriting was a miserable spastic-looking scrawl, and it too has remained that way for over half a century. Few people can decipher it, and I have trouble with it myself if I set it aside for a week and then come back to it. However, arithmetic was never much of a problem for me and reading has always been a breeze, starting with my first school-book called *Dickie Dare Goes to School* which I finished in one day even though it was supposed to occupy the first grade for several months. My speedy disposal of *Dickie Dare* is misleading because my mother had read it to me several times when Vic brought it home the year before I started school.

Our curriculum broadened during my second year to include some history, and this subject remained a part of our studies throughout grammar school. History, particularly during the first half of the 1920s, always emphasized the first of those three aspects of patriotism mentioned earlier: hatred of Germany.

In a variety of ways, mostly by word of mouth on the playgrounds, it became known to me that Germany was a wicked nation, and that all Germans were evil people, while Kaiser Wilhelm, or Kaiser Bill as we called him, was the most evil of them all. I learned he had ordered that the right hand of all French and Belgian boys in the territories Germany had conquered early in the war must be cut off to prevent them from later fighting against Germany. Also, his soldiers had attacked and mutilated all the nuns in the nunneries of occupied Belgium and France. There were no nunneries in south Dorchester, which was one hundred percent Methodist, and I had never seen a nun, so this second charge of German atrocities didn't bother me much, but the first did. Accordingly, I asked my father how a man could be so mean as to cut off the right hands of innocent little boys, and was relieved when he told me that Kaiser Bill had certainly done no such thing. It was propaganda, he said, to raise the level of patriotism, but he did add that both the Germans and the Allies had probably committed many real atrocities. He asked me which of my books had said that the Kaiser had chopped off the hands of boys and I told him that it was not in the books but I had heard it from my classmates and from many older boys.

Indeed, it was common knowledge in south Dorchester that the Germans were wicked enough to do anything, although the only printed material I can recall which supported this belief consisted of two pictures in one of our history books. The first of these two showed Kaiser Wilhelm in an arrogant pose sporting a full pointed beard and a mustache with its waxed ends pointing upward. Right beside this picture of the Kaiser was a drawing showing an almost identical face except that two horns were growing out above the ears. Apparently the Kaiser and the Devil were identical or at least identical twins.

While "brave little Belgium" was always given some favorable mention in our history books, France was the most heroic of the Allies—except, of course, the United States. The British were treated as respected and respectable cousins, but somehow they remained tainted, or tinted, by traces of red left over from the Redcoats who had fought George Washington a century and a half earlier. The French had no such problem. Lafayette had fought on the right side then, and when our brave soldiers had landed in France, they had all declared: "Lafayette, we are here." So Marshall Foch was second only to General Pershing in bravery and military wisdom.

However, this admiration of the French, while real and vibrant, was never as sharply focused as hatred of the Germans, even after my father told me that the hand chopping story was false. Moreover, hatred of the Germans was not such an ever-present thing in our history books as praise for the United States.

American statesmen of the 1920s, particularly Woodrow Wilson and his war relief administrator, Herbert Hoover, were all considered to be truly noble men, and our statesmen of the past were even more noble. Washington and Lincoln were the best of this generally incomparable group, but close behind them came Jefferson, Franklin, and Hamilton. Only Aaron Burr was tainted among the American statesmen. Benedict Arnold, of course, was much worse than Burr, but he had never been a real American—only a traitorous royalist bribed by George III. It would not have surprised me to learn that Arnold had been born a German.

Even my mother was caught up in the patriotic fervor right after World War I, but her enthusiasm was centered in her belief that Woodrow Wilson really had fought the war to end all wars. Consequently, she believed that Wilson was the greatest of all presidents—even better than Washington and Lincoln. My father thought otherwise and frequently said Wilson was a self-righteous snob who was almost as arrogant as the Kaiser. And to show that this was not a partisan political opinion rooted in the fact that Wilson was a Democrat, he said that Herbert Hoover was just as bad. My father's low opinion of Wilson and Hoover probably had a complex set of reasons behind it, but one factor surely was his resentment of the way

Fourth of July at Crapo

President Wilson and food administrator, Mr. Hoover, ran the food program during the last year of World War I. This program prevented my father from grinding enough of his own wheat into flour to fill the needs of his own table, and for this he never really forgave either man.

During the course of the 1920s patriotic fervor rather steadily declined in south Dorchester, as it probably did all over the nation, and by 1929 my opinion of both German and American statesmen had changed considerably. Many subliminal factors probably helped bring about the change in my thinking, but two important specific events were crucial in this process: first, a Fourth of July oration which my brother Conrad delivered in 1923 and, second, my father's sponsorship of Joe Gottlieb, a German immigrant who lived in our community for two years.

Which one of the many heavy blows that fell on Germany following World War I caused Mr. Gottlieb to leave his native land and come to the United States, I do not know. Nor do I know why he eventually came to south Dorchester, but the rumor was that he had tuberculosis, or consumption as we called it, and was seeking work on boats engaged in dredging for oysters in hope that the fresh air would improve his health. However, the boat captains would not employ him because he looked too frail for the work, and someone directed him to go see my father at the post office. Mr. Gottlieb had with him an even frailer-looking wife and two small children. He had no money, and his situation was such a desperate one that my father took pity on him and gave him a job cutting cordwood and other trees for lumbering purposes up in the largest of our three pine forests, near Farm Creek.

My father also arranged a seventy-five dollar loan at the bank for Mr. Gottlieb, and cosigned the note, so that his family had enough to make a down payment on a two-room house up near the pine forest, and to buy food with until he had earned some money by cutting wood. The Gottlieb family survived there for two years in what must have been a very hard life for all of them.

I remember that Mr. Gottlieb spoke excellent English,

27

much better than most of my neighbors did, even though he had a German accent. In fact his English was so good that he had trouble driving the oxen which he used in hauling out the larger trees from the woods. These oxen had been trained to respond to the command of "Huther" when the driver wanted them to come toward him. Mr. Gottlieb recognized that "huther" was a corruption of "hither" and that was the way he addressed them at first until my father told him that oxen didn't know what hither meant but did understand huther.

My father also told Mr. Gottlieb he should change his name to Godlove, which everyone in south Dorchester would respect, while they might resent Gottlieb because it would remind them of the fact that the Kaiser was reported to place himself above God by referring to "me und Gott." Very probably my father was thinking of the anti-German sentiment which had caused Baltimore to change German Street into Redwood Street during World War I, and in England caused Lord Battenberg to change his name to Mountbatten. In any event, there was never any resentment expressed against Mr. Gottlieb during his two-year stay in our community, and he did not have the slightest resemblance to what I had come to think of as the way a German was supposed to look or behave. Perhaps this was because the anti-German sentiment was receding everywhere or perhaps it was because the Gottliebs were such an obviously poor family. Mr. Gottlieb corresponded from time to time with some Germans living in Baltimore and after about two years moved his family there. When he left, he still had not been able to repay the seventy-five dollars which he had borrowed from the bank, so my father, as cosigner of the note, had to make it good. My father never complained about this, saying Mr. Gottlieb was a decent, honest man who had done the best he could under very difficult circumstances. Mr. Gottlieb drastically altered my opinion of Germans and Germany.

However, the Fourth of July oration which Conrad delivered at Crapo in 1923 did even more to change my views about foreign nations. Crapo, originally called Woodlandtown, was renamed in honor of William Wallace Crapo, a

Fourth of July at Crapo

Massachusetts lawyer and Republican who served in the United States House of Representatives when James A. Garfield was majority leader of the House. Mr. Crapo and Garfield were friends and when, in January 1880, Garfield was elected by the Ohio state legislature to become a United States Senator, effective March 4, 1881, he persuaded Postmaster General Horace Maynard to name a post office in honor of his friend. Garfield was a uniquely influential man in 1880 because he was not only a United States Senator-elect, but later that year became President-elect of the United States. Crapo lived much longer than his friend, Garfield, and died at age ninety-six in 1926, but there is nothing in the record to indicate that he ever visited the post office named in his honor.

The people who live in Crapo pronounce it "Cray-po," but strangers often laugh and call it "Crap-o." It was chosen for the Fourth of July celebration in south Dorchester during the 1920s because it is near the geographic center of the seven small towns which lay south of the Blackwater River: Andrews, Lakesville, Crapo, Wingate, Toddsville, Bishops Head, and Crocheron. The celebrations were held on the church grounds overlooking a village square formed by the high school and Red Men's Hall on one side of the road, facing the Methodist Church, parsonage, and Kirwan's carpentry shop on the other side. The program for these celebrations varied from year to year but usually included an oyster supper for adults, ice cream cones for children, plus games and entertainment of one sort or another for everyone. One year a trumpet player from Cambridge attempted to play both taps and "The Star-Spangled Banner." He got by satisfactorily with taps but had to stop several times before he finally battered his way through the national anthem.

Regardless of all annual variations in the Fourth of July celebrations at Crapo, the feature event was always an oration, usually delivered by a visiting politician or preacher. However, in 1922 and 1923 my brother Conrad was the orator. Why Conrad, who was still in college, was chosen in 1922 I do not know, but his first effort was such a smashing success that he was immediately engaged to be the orator again in 1923.

29

Before the Bridge

Conrad's first oration consisted of his recital of Robert William Service's World War I poem "Jean Desprez." The poem starts out, mildly enough, this way:

> Oh ye whose hearts are resonant, and ring the
> War's romance,
> Hear ye the story of a boy, a peasant boy of
> France.

But the second verse really sets the tone of this poem which Service wrote when he, like so many others, was caught up in the full fury of anti-German fervor.

> With fire and sword the Teuton horde was
> ravaging the land,
> And there was darkness and despair, grim death
> on every hand;
> Red fields of slaughter sloping down to ruin's
> black abyss;
> The wolves of war ran evil-fanged, and little
> did they miss.
> And on they came with fear and flame, to burn
> and loot and slay,
> Until they reached the red-roofed croft, the
> house of Jean Desprez.

The poem continued for a total of twelve verses, all in the same purple vein, and so it is not necessary to do more than give a brief summary of the story.

When the German army reached the village where Jean Desprez lived, some defender shot and killed a member of the invading army. Whereupon, the captain of the company which had suffered the casualty gathered together all the men of the village, selected ten of them, lined them up against the church wall, and shot them all to death in front of their terrified relatives and neighbors.

Fourth of July at Crapo

A wounded French soldier—a Zouave—lying in a ditch saw all this and decided to do what he could to even the score and so he shot the German captain who fell beside "his victims ten."

The fury of the Germans then reached new heights. They dragged the wounded Zouave from his ditch and prepared to shoot and club him to death until the German major, next in line above the fallen captain, had a better idea. The major directed his soldiers to crucify the Zouave, who was then promptly pinned with bayonets to the church door and left to hang there until he died. This brave French hero was pre-pared to die, but before he died he begged for some water—"a single drop he cried," but the Germans mocked him with an empty cup and "saw his eye grow dim."

No villager dared offer the dying man the drop of water he begged for until suddenly Jean Desprez, too young to be in the army but not too young to be a hero, suddenly walked up and "gave the drink to him."

Again the Germans flew into a frenzy and were about to shoot young Jean Desprez until, once again, the German ma-jor had another of his better ideas. Let the young peasant save his own life by killing the poor wretch he had just befriended. It would, the major said, show to all what craven dogs the French were.

So they placed Jean Desprez in front of the dying Zouave, put a German rifle in his hands, made him understand what he had to do, and gave him one minute to do it. During that one minute the sweetness of French farm life, the glories of French history, and a host of other things flashed through the young peasant boy's mind, while all around him he heard the sounds of "shoot!" Even the dying Zouave said, "shoot!" because it would be best for both of them.

> "'Shoot! Shoot!" the dying Zouave moaned;
> "Shoot! Shoot!" the soldiers said.
> And Jean Desprez reached out and shot . . .
> *The Prussian major dead!*

Before the Bridge

Conrad recited this long and lurid poem slowly, allowing the pathos to sink into the minds of his audience, and when he got to those last four words, he stopped entirely for perhaps two seconds. When the final four words came, they hit the crowd like a bombshell, and the round of applause which followed set a record for all Fourth of July celebrations at Crapo.

It never occurred to me or the rest of Conrad's audience to think about what must have happened to Jean Desprez and his relatives and neighbors after he fired that heroic shot. In fact, when I learned that Conrad had been invited back to be the orator again in 1923, I rather hoped he would have a sequel telling how some German colonel or even a general had also been confounded.

But he did not. Perhaps the reaction of his 1922 audience shook him as much as it pleased him. Anyway, in 1923 he wrote his own oration, and it was a sober appeal to his listeners to forget the romance of war and think only of its tragic and unheroic side. He said that our allies in the late war were not without fault and never had been. Even the United States was not faultless.

First he said that France's greatest hero, Napoleon, had invaded more nations and had left deeper and wider rivers of blood, with as many starving widows and children scattered in the wake of his conquering armies as the Kaiser had left in Belgium and France. Then he said the British had not obtained possession of nearly half the world by gentle persuasion only. They had fought the Boers in their home territory in Africa, the Indians in India, the natives in Australia, and even George Washington in the United States.

All this sobered me and the rest of his audience somewhat, but he shook us to our roots when he went on to say that even the United States had not always fought nobly. He pointed out that Americans had fought each other during the Civil War and so all of them could not be just and noble, and he concluded by saying that one great hero of the Civil War, General Grant, had said that even our war with Mexico was not entirely a just war.

Fourth of July at Crapo

Conrad received only mild applause when he finished this oration and he was not invited back for 1924. It was many years later before I read exactly what General Grant had said about the Mexican war. He wrote in his *Personal Memoirs* that the Mexican war was one of the most unjust ever waged by a stronger against a weaker nation. In retrospect, it seems to me that Conrad was wise not to give General Grant's exact words about the Mexican war. If he had done so, he might not have received any applause at all.

All this occurred long before World War II when our bitter enemies, Germany and Japan, became trusted friends soon after the war ended, but Conrad's speech did start me to thinking about how difficult it is to separate the heroes from the villains when war comes. It is all nearly as confusing as it was when Miss Andrews put mosquitoes on the bottom of the protein food chain, and Dr. Tawes promptly reversed the order and put mosquitoes on the top—right above people.

FOUR

Cambridge and the Jail House

IN looking back, I cannot say for certain whether the fields, forests, rivers, or marshes of Dorchester taught me the most about biology and ecology. I lean toward the marshes, but a good case can also be made for each of the other three.

There is no question, however, about where I learned the most about the accoutrements and embellishments of civilization as it flourished during the 1920s. It was Cambridge, the seat of the Eastern Shore's largest county. But Cambridge was not just a county seat. At that time it was also the undisputed queen city of the entire Eastern Shore of Maryland. Cambridge not only had a larger population than any other town on the Shore, but it also had a greater variety of industries, services, and related activities.

Unlike the up-to-date Kansas City immortalized by Rodgers and Hammerstein in *Oklahoma!* it had no seven-story skyscrapers and no burlesque theatres, but it did have a number of things which Kansas City could not claim, such as a pier for oceangoing vessels, and blue crabs swimming under the bridge which connected East Cambridge with the rest of the town.

It also had a fairgrounds and a professional baseball park, a jail, an armory, a railroad station and a bus depot, a library and two newspapers equipped with linotype machines and power presses, a hospital, a plant to manufacture ice, a poolroom and a bowling alley, two movie houses, three hotels, an assortment of public eating places, including the only one in Maryland that served steamed oysters, the largest tomato cannery in the state, a tin can fabricating plant, two boatyards and an iron working plant that made oyster dredges, and a hun-

34

Cambridge and the Jail House

dred or so shops and stores, including a hardware store which was so modern that it had a pneumatic tube system for speeding money back and forth between salesmen on the main floor and a treasurer located on the mezzanine floor.

In addition to all this the older boys often hinted darkly to us younger ones that Cambridge had two bordellos—one on the east side and another on the west side. This wickedly intriguing bit of information probably reflected nothing except the tendency of boys who have passed the age of puberty to brag and let on that they are devilish fellows who know their way around the world. If there really were any bordellos in Cambridge, they were always managed with so much discretion that no candidate for mayor or sheriff ever campaigned on the promise to root them out if he got elected. But if the painted women of Cambridge were imaginary or at worst amateurs, as the French say, the people associated with all the other things mentioned above were real enough and always present in Cambridge, particularly on Saturday nights when they were joined by still others drawn in from the far reaches of Dorchester.

In fact, Cambridge grew about one-fifth in population every Saturday because it was a long established custom, during the 1920s, for the residents of all the outlying districts of Dorchester to "go to town" once a week—to shop in Cambridge's many stores, to see each other, and generally to enjoy the delights of city life. Watermen from Hooper Island, Elliott Island, Toddville, Wingate, Bishops Head, Hill's Point, and Secretary stopped their pursuit of crabs and oysters to mingle with farmers from Vienna, East New Market, and Hurlock, trappers from Andrews and other points along the Blackwater River, and with plumbers and electricians from Cambridge itself.

There were no plumbers and electricians from the outlying districts because there was no plumbing or electricity in these places. But there were politicians from all over the county in Cambridge on Saturday nights because Dorchester was celebrated for its political clout in those days. Cambridge, during the previous decade, had produced two governors of

35

Before the Bridge

Maryland—Phillips Lee Goldsborough, a Republican, and Emerson P. Harrington, a Democrat, and both of them were still potent factors in the political life of Maryland. My father seldom visited Cambridge on Saturday nights during the 1920s, but when he did, he never failed to hold long discussions with political friends even though he had retired from active politics a decade or so earlier.

Vic and I went to Cambridge every Saturday if we could find free transportation or could rustle up enough money to pay our way on Albert Kirwan's bus and still have enough left to sample the glitter of Cambridge's many attractions. At one time or another we became familiar with all of them even though the movie houses, the poolroom, and the baseball park were our favorite spots. But before I got to know any of these fascinating places, I was introduced to the Cambridge Hospital.

This introduction, which also gave me my first taste of organic chemistry, came about because I stuck a rusty nail in my bare foot while running through Insley's canning factory at Wingate. My foot became infected and swelled so alarmingly that my father took me to see his long-time friend, Dr. Brice W. Goldsborough, brother of Governor Goldsborough and chief surgeon at the hospital. Dr. Goldsborough was such a skillful surgeon that he was accepted as both a professional peer and personal friend of Dr. Howard A. Kelly, one of the Big Four at the Johns Hopkins Hospital in Baltimore. The two surgeons often went on camping trips to such places as Canada and Mexico.

Dr. Goldsborough took one look at my swollen foot and decided it needed surgery. Whereupon he had me rolled into the operating room at the hospital and anaesthetized with diethyl ether, after which he lanced and drained the swollen foot. The thing I remember most vividly about the whole affair was how sick I was after I regained consciousness.

I did not know it then, but a half-century dispute about the relative merits of diethyl ether and chloroform as an anaesthetic had recently been resolved in favor of ether when I made my first visit to the Cambridge Hospital. It had been

Cambridge and the Jail House

known from the very beginning that ether tended to leave the recovering patient very nauseated while chloroform was only slightly objectionable in that respect. But during the early 1920s it became known that chloroform caused liver damage and so the decision went against chloroform. Nevertheless, if I had been given a vote while I was still sick from that ether, I surely would have voted for chloroform.

In any event, diethyl ether remained the preferred anaesthetic in hospitals for another twenty-five years until it was finally replaced by a chemical known as Fluothane, invented by Dr. Charles Suckling, an Englishman working for the English firm called ICI. It was my pleasure to arrange, in 1982, to have Dr. Suckling deliver the principal address at Washington College's "Two Hundred Years of Chemistry," one of the programs which the college staged as a part of its bicentennial celebration. After Dr. Suckling finished his address, I told him that he had made his discovery too late to save me two very uncomfortable hours back in 1921. He apologized.

While my first taste of organic chemistry was distinctly unpleasant, my introduction to physical chemistry, which came a few years later, was not unpleasant at all—merely puzzling. This introduction to physical chemistry came from the ice-making plant in Cambridge.

I had marvelled to John Burrs, my father's farmhand, about the miracle of summer ice when he and I had seen large cakes of it on the steamboat pier at Wingate one hot July day. John told me that while that particular ice may have been made in Baltimore there also was an ice-making plant in Cambridge and that his cousin worked at the ice plant, where they made ice during the summer months by the simple process of putting pressure on water.

"They squeeze the water," John said, "until it changes to ice. They have a big compressor run by a steam engine to generate the pressure needed to squeeze the water."

John's explanation of how ice was manufactured in hot weather by putting pressure on water had never been very satisfying, and I had gone to my father for further explanation. My father said John had left out a few critical details.

37

"They do have a compressor, but they don't use it to squeeze water. They compress ammonia to change it from a gas to a liquid, and then when the liquid ammonia is allowed to evaporate, it takes up heat and cools the water until finally the water gets so cold it freezes. The ammonia keeps going in a circle first from a liquid to gas—thereby cooling the water—and then the gas is compressed back to a liquid again, after which it evaporates once again doing still more cooling."

My father's explanation made it clear to me that ice did not form simply by putting pressure on water, as John had said, but even my father's explanation left me feeling far from sure that I knew how ice was really made during hot weather. I said so, and he told me to visit the ice plant some day when I was in Cambridge. However, when I visited the ice plant, I still came away puzzled as to what the heavy equipment there was really doing. The operators running the compressor and the "brine room" didn't seem to know much more about it than John did. The only new thing I really learned was that the evaporating ammonia first cools a tank of salt water which is kept from freezing by having salt dissolved in it. This very cold brine solution is then pumped around the containers which hold the fresh water that is to be frozen into the big cakes I had seen at the steamboat wharf. The evaporating ammonia and the brine solution which stayed liquid even when fresh water froze were both lessons in physical chemistry, but they remained puzzles to me for many years to come.

However, the professional ball park at Cambridge which did so much to encourage our interest in baseball was a source of great pleasure and satisfaction to Vic and me. Baseball, indirectly, was what gave Vic and me an understanding of how the Cambridge jail really operated.

During the 1920s baseball was intensely interesting to just about everyone in Dorchester except my father who thought all atheletic contests were a boring waste of time. My mother was not much of a fan either, but she did read the occasional pieces on baseball which Wilson, my oldest brother, wrote for

Cambridge and the Jail House

the *Baltimore Sun* even though he specialized in football and lacrosse.

In fact, baseball was the favorite sport for all of Maryland during the 1920s, and the reasons for this were obvious. Babe Ruth was at the peak of his fame as a slugger, and every time he hit a home run he created a new record. The Babe was playing for the New York Yankees then, but he had been born in Baltimore and played his first professional baseball for the Baltimore Orioles so all of Maryland looked on him as one of their own. His big moon-shaped face was far better known than any other in the nation, including that of President Calvin Coolidge. Also, the Babe's predecessor as home run king of baseball was also a Marylander—Frank "Home Run" Baker who had played for the Philadelphia Athletics when they were world champions. Baker had retired from the Athletics by the 1920s and was living on his farm at Trappe, Maryland just across the Choptank River, in Talbot County.

All this was exciting to baseball fans in Dorchester County, but the thing which really got them steaming hot was Cambridge's own professional baseball team, the Canners, named in honor of the county's largest employer, the Phillips Packing Company. The Canners played in the Class D Eastern Shore Baseball League which also included towns in three states: Maryland, Delaware, and Virginia. The pennant winner in this Eastern Shore League annually played in a Little World Series against the champion of the Blue Ridge League on the western side of the Chesapeake Bay. The towns in the Blue Ridge League were located in Maryland, Pennsylvania, and West Virginia and so the series between the Eastern Shore League and the Blue Ridge League champions was called the Five State Series by the *Baltimore Sun*. The name of Little World Series was reserved by the *Sun* for the series between the winner in the International League (usually Baltimore) and the champion of the American Association.

In 1925 the Cambridge Canners won the pennant in the Eastern Shore League and thus had the honor of playing Hagerstown, winner in the Blue Ridge League, for the championship in the Five State Series. All Dorchester promptly entered into a state of euphoria which lasted for ten days and seven games, ending only when Hagerstown won the seventh and final game, played on the neutral ground of Oriole Park in Baltimore.

This ultimate failure by the Cambridge Canners was a devastating blow to Vic, Mark, and me, but we soon recovered and began looking ahead to next year. In fact, by 1928 when Vic and I were juniors in high school, local contests in south Dorchester were more important to us than any professional games because we played in these hometown games. I played third base for the Crapo High School team and also sometimes played that same position for the Crapo town team or men's team as we usually called it. Vic, who was the star of our high school team because of his hitting ability, was always assured of a starting position on the town team, but I only was a "fill in" player.

Neither the high school team nor the town team had any scheduled program of games. The Crapo High School team played a home game series with the Hooper Island High School team and that ended our season, but the town team played throughout the summer whenever we could schedule games with Toddville, Bishops Head, Lakesville, Hooper Island, or Cambridge. This scheduling really was a hit-or-miss thing usually arranged by our first baseman, a man whom I shall call Ross because that was not his name.

Ross was by a wide margin the oldest man on our town team. He was perhaps thirty-five or forty years old while the rest of us were only fifteen to twenty. The fact that Ross still wanted to play baseball at his age gives some indication of the sort of man he was, a free spirit who resolutely refused to bow down to the dictates of polite society or even those of the law. He held no regular job but earned his living by a whole series of entrepreneurial activities which ranged from selling Sunday newspapers to butchering hogs and bootlegging whiskey.

Bootlegging of whiskey was illegal all over the nation during the 1920s and was against the local laws even before national prohibition because south Dorchester had been dry

Cambridge and the Jail House

by local option for a long time. Nevertheless, there had always been a demand for whiskey in south Dorchester and, as is usually the case, where a demand exists, suppliers come forward. These suppliers were not given hearty approval by the community as a whole but neither were they social outcasts. I remember that one of the younger members of our high school baseball team told me when I came home from college one year that he had dropped out of school and had his own crabbing boat.

"Crabbing is my official business, but once a week I run over to St. Mary's County to pick up a boat load of whiskey, and I make more money that one day than I do crabbing the rest of the week."

Bootlegging was a profitable business in those days and even had social status attached to it in certain circles. It was widely reported that Maryland's governor during the 1920s, the distinguished looking Albert C. Ritchie, saw nothing wrong with it and dealt with the higher class bootleggers regularly whenever his stocks grew depleted. Anyway, it probably was the most profitable of Ross's many entrepreneurial ventures; it gave him contacts all over the county, and he used these contacts to schedule baseball games for the town teams.

Most of Crapo's baseball games were played against nearby towns and villages such as Toddville, Bishops Head, and Hooper Island where travel was not much of a problem. Ross would run into representatives in the sporting set of these locations and schedule a game with them for the coming week, or some other time which was mutually convenient. On rare occasions our team at Crapo played Cambridge. That is to say, we played a pick-up team chosen from the area around the Phillips Packing Company because Ross knew enough of the young baseball enthusiasts living there to assemble nine players. If we won, we told ourselves that we had defeated the team representing a town ten times our size, and if we lost, we had a good excuse.

The most distant team which Ross ever scheduled us to play was the team from Hills Point or "Hills Pint," as Ross called it. Hills Point was right at the top of the peninsula lying between the Choptank and Little Choptank rivers. By air it was no farther from Crapo than Cambridge was, but by land it was nearly twice as far. This was because it was necessary first to drive up the neck peninsula from Hills Point to Cambridge and then down the peninsula formed by the Honga and Nanticoke rivers to Crapo.

Ross ran into some sportsmen from Hills Point in Cambridge on one of his Saturday night visits and challenged them to a baseball game to be played at Crapo on the coming Wednesday. They accepted, and both parties agreed that next Wednesday would allow ample time for the assembling of the two teams. Vic was naturally included in the Crapo team, and even I seemed assured of a starting position because our regular third baseman had taken a job in Crisfield and had been away for a month.

Anyway, the Crapo team assembled at Bradford's baseball field well before the 2:00 P.M. starting time which Ross said he had agreed upon. We held our warm-up practice before 1:45 and were only slightly concerned when no visiting team had put in an appearance by the scheduled game time.

"The Hills Pint team," Ross said, "may have had a flat tire or maybe they took a wrong turn and went part of the way to Hooper Island. But don't worry, they'll be here."

However, by 2:30 we were all beginning to worry because there was still no sign of a Hills Point team. We took another warm-up practice and then sat down under a big tree. The discussion was rather dispirited because it was slowly becoming evident that we probably had been stood up. Ross, however, insisted that Hills Point would eventually show up, and he took over the conversation in an effort to keep the rest of us from deciding to give up and go home.

"You young guys have got to learn how to wait, something I learned how to do when I was in jail."

We all knew that Ross had been caught by the prohibition agents in one of his bootlegging projects a couple of years ago and had spent ninety days in the Cambridge jail but I had always assumed that he was sensitive about the matter and didn't want to talk about it. But when he brought the subject up himself I asked him what it was like to spend time in jail.

"Why do you want to know?" he asked, fixing me with that piercing eye which he turned upon anyone who attracted his full attention. He had a hawk-like face which resembled Prince Philip's of England, except that his eyes were more intense than Philip's. I said rather lamely that I had no particular reason for asking about the jail and that caused Ross to relax, and he began to talk freely about it.

"It was awful damn dull in jail except when they threw a new prisoner in with us. This happened only once or twice a week although we usually had at least one every Saturday night. That always created a little excitement for a few hours."

"Why was that exciting?" one of his listeners asked Ross.

"Because as soon as the jailer left we assembled our kangaroo court and tried the new prisoner for disturbing the peace of our jail. We had a judge, a prosecuting attorney, a defense attorney, and a jury made up of whoever was left over. Then we went through the whole rigamarole of a trial with the defense attorney declaring that the new guy was innocent, or too young, or too old, to stand trial, but the result was always the same. We found him guilty and fined him whatever sum of money he had on him. Then we took the fine money and gave it to one of the jail attendants and asked him to go out and buy soft drinks, cokes, and candy bars for all of us."

"What happened if the new prisoner wouldn't recognize the authority of your court and refused to give up all his money?"

"We all jumped on him, beat the hell out of him, and took the money anyway."

"Didn't he call to the jailer for help?"

"Some of them did but it didn't do 'em a damn bit of good because the jailer always got his share of the soft drinks and candy so he never interfered with our court. Actually, we never got much money from any one guy—usually twenty-five or fifty cents. I think the biggest fine we ever collected was about seven dollars and forty cents. Half the time the guy didn't have a damn cent so we sentenced him to clean up the main lobby where we held court and anybody's cell that needed it. Some other times we beat the hell out of him just for something to do."

Ross made it all sound rather funny, but even at the time it occurred to me that it couldn't have seemed very funny to the new guy.

"How was the food in jail?"

"Lousy as hell. That's why we always wanted to send out for something to eat and drink. The damn food wasn't no good to start with, and by the time the jail cook got finished slopping it around no self-respecting dog would want to eat it."

"Did anything pleasant ever happen in jail?" I asked Ross.

"I already told you that the most pleasant thing was when they threw a new guy in with us," he answered.

Then he paused for a moment before saying: "Well, it sometimes was pleasant on Sunday mornings. We had a rule that everybody had to dress up in his best clothes on Sunday. Some guys, of course, didn't have no clothes except what they had on their backs, but even they were required to wash their faces and brush their hair. Sometimes the new guys who had been thrown in the night before didn't want to do it, but they always did as soon as we explained the rules to them."

Ross paused at this point, a wicked grin creased his face, and he obviously was inviting another question. Therefore, one of us asked how they explained the rules.

"We all jumped on the S.O.B. and beat the hell out of him, and after that he never caused us no more trouble."

By the time Ross finished his story about jail life it was clear to me that the most entertaining and interesting thing that went on there was beating the hell out of some new prisoner. Also, by the time Ross had finished his account of jail life it was about 3:30, and since all of us, Ross included, were sure that the Hills Point baseball team was not going to show up, we all went home.

That weekend Wilson drove home from Baltimore in his Moon automobile, for one of his brief visits, and while we were eating his favorite food of green peas and new potatoes, he

44

Cambridge and the Jail House

asked Vic and me if we had played any baseball games lately. We told him we had beaten Toddville a week ago but that Hills Point had failed to show up for a scheduled game on Wednesday.

"Well," Wilson told us, "after the home team waits a reasonable time and the visiting team still doesn't show up, the home team is entitled to claim the game by forfeit; the record shows the home team winning by a nine to nothing score. Why don't you wait another week or so, and if Hills Point still hasn't put in an appearance, you can claim a victory by forfeit."

Well, that was all about fifty years ago, and so far as I know Hills Point hasn't shown up yet. Accordingly, I now claim a victory by forfeit—

Crapo	9
Hills Point	0

Nunc Pro Tunc

THERE may have been a time when I had trouble deciding whether to say "They invited my brother and me" or "They invited my brother and I"; but if so it was so long ago that I can't remember it. Nor can I remember who or what persuaded me that it should be "me" instead of "I."

Perhaps it was because of what I heard at home or maybe it was something said to me by my two young and beautiful English teachers—the blonde Miss Hope Dorman in my first year of high school or the red-haired Miss Dorothy Purdum in my senior year. They both spoke flawless English, but if they said anything to me about "me" and "I," it has vanished into the mists of time.

Professor Bergen Evans and other experts on speech have noted that children teach each other how to speak, on the playground and other places, and there surely is a lot of truth in this claim. The children may not make any conscious effort to instruct each other, but they do so anyway by ridiculing anyone who uses grammar not approved by the majority. I'm sure there would have been snickers and snorts of derision on the playground at Crapo High School if I had said, "They invited my brother and I," but there would have been no objection to "my brother and me."

Today, of course, television reporters, Ph.D. chemists, and a host of other educated people think "They invited my brother and I" is the proper way to say it, but on the playground at Crapo during the 1920s such talk would have been hooted at—as intolerable affectation, not necessarily bad grammar. During the 1920s at Crapo High School we had such a fondness for the objective case that the most readily accepted constructions would have been "me and my brother were invited" or "me and my brother was invited." Even today no one gets it wrong if only one person is invited, because television reporters and all others avoid saying "They invited I."

During the past half century I have drifted away from many expressions which were standard in south Dorchester in those days, and now I feel quite comfortable saying "This is he" when someone asks for me on the telephone, but it still seems odd to say "It is I" when I knock on a door and someone asks who is there. So I always say "It's me" unless I am calling on English teachers or other members of the educationally elite.

As I said earlier, I do not know how or why all this came about, but my two sisters, Evelyn and Carolyn, have a simple explanation for it: Latin. Their theory is that anyone who studies Latin in his formative years is automatically and irresistibly pushed along the road toward good grammar in English. Latin, they say, benefits its students in ways which are important even though the poor student may not be aware of what is happening at the time, and then they point out that Latin was the keystone of the curriculum at Crapo High School when I was a student there during the 1920s.

The last part of the sentence above is certainly true even though the first part may be debatable. Latin was the keystone of my high school studies. It was taught by the school principal, Emory Augustus Coughlin, Sr., and every student was required to take two years of Latin whether he planned to go to college or drop out of school as soon as the law permitted. Mr. Coughlin's enthusiasm for Latin was boundless and much of this enthusiasm was absorbed by his students who were forced to be grammatically correct in Latin no matter how distorted their English might be. He never defended Latin or said that it disciplined the mind, ordered thinking, or did any of the other things which Latin enthusiasts have claimed for it over the years. He simply took it for granted that everyone recognized the supreme importance of Latin, and if its other proponents had behaved similarly Latin might still be flourishing in high schools today. But they did not.

After the Romans quit speaking Latin and went over to its first cousin, Italian, the language of the Caesars would have vanished entirely except for the fact that it was kept alive in the monasteries and a few other European enclaves of learning during the Dark Ages. There it managed to survive for several hundred years, feeding on the belief that scholars needed a well defined and unchanging language in which to record their discoveries and philosophies. By the time Columbus discovered America, Latin was well established in Europe as the language of scholars, and it came over to the new world on that basis.

As soon as they had developed a small measure of security against starvation and the Indian menace, some of the colonists began to thirst for the scholarly life and accordingly encouraged the importation of a few Latin scholars from England. These scholars trained others in Latin, and soon the language of Caesar was to be found in all the fledgling colleges of America. These Latin experts were dedicated to making scholars of all Americans, and to a very small extent they succeeded. That is to say, about one-half of one percent of all Americans learned how to speak and write Latin. But this tiny minority persuaded the great unwashed majority that if a man wished to be counted among the educated, he must speak and write Latin. This was particularly true for clergymen, lawyers, and doctors, from the time of the Revolutionary War up to slightly beyond the Civil War.

If a lawyer did not know how to draw up a writ of habeas corpus, he was not accepted in the legal fraternity, and if a doctor didn't know how to write out a prescription for nux vomica, he was looked upon as more like a witch doctor than a physician. Futhermore, clergymen who didn't know that A.D. meant anno Domini or the year of the Lord were likely to be travelling evangelists instead of settled comfortably in a wealthy parish.

Nunc Pro Tunc

At least that is the way things were until after the Civil War. Before that time the average American had been so busy trying to grub a living out of the wilderness that he had no time at all for Latin and not much more for his own language which he usually spoke in a freewheeling style that offended protectors of the King's English almost as much as it horrified Latin scholars. But during the period from 1860 to 1900 this average American, having been thrown in contact with some of the Latin scholars on the battlefield, began to lose some of his respect for them and to wonder if Latin was all it was cracked up to be.

Why couldn't a judge say "have the body in court" instead of writing out a writ of habeas corpus, and why shouldn't he say "now for then" instead of nunc pro tunc? Also, why couldn't the doctor prescribe a dose of vomiting nut instead of nux vomica when his patient swallowed something the doctor thought he had better disgorge? These examples of heretical thinking became more and more frequent as the laws of the land and pharmacopoeia grew constantly more complicated, thereby giving lawyers and doctors an ample supply of terms to use in confusing their clients and patients without having to resort to Latin. All this did not change the doctors and lawyers who kept right on using Latin anyway, but it did have an effect on Latin itself; slowly its use began to diminish in American life.

The retreat of Latin in formal learning was accelerated after 1900 when American colleges and universities began to import scholars from Germany. These scholars let it be known that they had long been recording their findings in German, instead of Latin, without any loss in precision. In fact, the Germans said that use of their native tongue, in place of Latin, had speeded up the dissemination of useful knowledge instead of impeding it. As a consequence of this and many other factors, by 1920 Latin had been driven from the academic field entirely in many places in American and was in full retreat in most others.

But Crapo High School was a firm exception. Latin was not

in retreat there; it retained its central position in the curriculum throughout my high school years. For one reason or another, I read a lot of books during high school, ranging from Nick Carter detective stories to Mark Twain and Shakespeare, but I learned nothing at all about physics and chemistry and not much more about mathematics, even though I had courses in algebra, geometry, and trigonometry.

In algebra I learned how to solve simple algebraic equations but not how to set up the equation from an English sentence defining the problem. For example, I could not write the equation which should be set up to solve a riddle which says: "I am thinking of a number such that five times the number, less four, equals three times the number plus ten. What is the number?" My father could do such puzzles in his head in a few seconds, but I never learned how to figure out such things until after I started college algebra.

My ability to make use of geometry was equally slight, but I did learn from Mr. Coughlin that Q.E.D., which appeared at the end of each theorem, stood for the Latin phrase: quod erat demonstrandum. My understanding of trigonometry was even weaker than my ability to apply algebra and geometry. I knew that the secant was the reciprocal of the cosine, and the cotangent was the reciprocal of the tangent, but how this information might be put to use was a complete mystery to me.

Consequently, I have always been skeptical that a knowledge of Latin grammar and Caesar's Gallic Wars fully compensated for the things I might have learned in high school but did not. Nevertheless, it does seem to me that there is an entertaining and sometimes useful comradery among those who have studied Latin. There probably were elements of snobbery in this comradery during the period before 1900, but today it appears to be something like the kinship felt by those who have learned some difficult but seldom used skill such as how to throw a boomerang, rope a steer, or sing all the words in the "Major-General's Song" from *The Pirates of Penzance.*

I first encountered this tendency on the part of all Latin students to welcome fellow sufferers into the clan when I was a sophomore studying solid analytical geometry at Washington College. On one test paper I finished a theorem proving that the intersection of a plane with a sphere was a circle by writing: Quod Erat Demonstrandum at the end of my proof. The teacher of this course was Dr. J. S. W. Jones, Dean of the College and famous as a stern taskmaster. When he returned the papers, he asked me to stop by his desk after the class was over.

"Why did you write 'Quod Erat Demonstrandum' after your proof instead of Q.E.D.?"

"Because that is what Q.E.D. means."

"Do you know what it means in English?"

"Of course; it means 'what was to be demonstrated'."

The Dean beamed and from that point on seemed to have a new respect for me. He said that Latin was one of his hobbies, and thereafter when we met in the halls or on the campus, we often threw Latin phrases at each other.

One day Bill Dannenberg, a junior and one of the dean's star mathematics students, overheard us in one of these exchanges and grabbed me by the arm until the dean had moved on.

"Be careful, Wingate. All of us majoring in mathematics have a slogan which we apply to the Old Boy. We say: 'Non illegitimus carborundum est'."

"What does that mean?" I asked, but Dannenberg grinned and said, "You are so damn smart in Latin I'll let you figure it out, but I will tell you that you won't find carborundum in any Latin dictionary."

He was right about that, and I had to come back to him for a translation.

"Carborundum sounds like Latin, but it really is a trademark name for silicon carbide which is a material so hard that it is used as an abrasive in grinding wheels. Now do you get it?"

I said I still did not, and so he continued: "Don't tell the Old Boy but a liberal translation says: 'Don't let the bastard wear you down'."

Dannenberg and I often used the expression when we met during the next two years, but I never saw it in print until 1982

Before the Bridge

when the *Washington Post* published a piece under that headline. The *Post* piece rambled on about Latin for a column or so but never did get around to translating its heading. This proves, I suppose, that Cole Porter was wrong in 1934 when he wrote a song saying "Anything Goes." Apparently in a family newspaper, even today, there are some things which do not go. However, I have a feeling that the author of the *Post*'s essay enjoyed himself far more than he would have if he had been writing about the cosine or the secant.

And so did Ambrose Bierce in his *Devil's Dictionary* when he noted that belladonna means a deadly poison in English but beautiful lady in Italian. Bierce said that it was a striking example of the essential identity of the two tongues. Nevertheless, whenever I am inclined to accept the thesis of my two sisters that Latin is worth all the time I ever spent on it, the phrase caveat emptor also invariably comes to mind.

Washington College and Bushrod

MY oldest brother, Wilson, started college in 1913 and my youngest brother, Mark, graduated from college in 1938. In between these two dates my parents arranged to send their other five children—Evelyn, Conrad, Carolyn, Vic, and me—through college also. All of which meant that my father had his nose pressed hard against the grindstone for a quarter of a century, and my mother was forced to scrimp and save just about everything she saw around her except perhaps the loose sand from that grindstone.

Whether my parents thought the results were worth all their time and hard work I can't say for certain but they never once faltered in their efforts to support their offspring during this long academic binge, and they also successfully encouraged their older children to help pay the college bills of the younger ones. In time, their progeny collected a total of twelve college degrees—all from Maryland institutions except one. Evelyn sneaked over to George Washington University in the District of Columbia for her Ph.D. in English.

Washington College in Chestertown came closest to being alma mater for all the Wingates because four of them—Conrad, Carolyn, Mark, and I—graduated there, and Wilson went there for one year, before he obtained a scholarship at Western Maryland where he graduated.

When Vic and I were seniors in high school, we both applied for admission to Washington College, and both of us were accepted. However, Vic subsequently was given a partial athletic scholarship by Curley Byrd at the University of Maryland and accordingly enrolled at College Park. I was sufficiently aware of how tight finances would be for four years in

the Wingate family, with two children in college at the same
time, to be glad Vic had received the scholarship, but I was also
glad that it was Vic who was going to the University of Maryland instead of me.

This was because I had become convinced that Washington College was just about the most glamorous place a college
student could hope to be. This 1929 notion of mine had
developed over a period of about six years and grew out of a
lot of things, most of them associated with the fact that Conrad
had graduated there in 1923 and Carolyn in 1929. I doubt that
either one of them intended to convey the impression which I
picked up, but they did nevertheless. Conrad caused me to
believe that the college was populated, in both the student
body and faculty, with people who were filled with idealism
and noble aspirations while Carolyn's accounts of college life
gave me the impression that the students there were highly
sophisticated and intellectual.

Carolyn has vigorously denied, from time to time during
the intervening years, that she ever had any such notions
herself or ever gave me any reasonable cause for thinking that
she did, but nevertheless that is what I believed in 1929. That
year produced the very last yell of the roaring twenties, and
Carolyn had been, for several years, bringing home pictures of
fellow students who displayed all the accoutrements of that
golden age before the stock market crash—girls with bobbed
hair, short skirts, and rolled hose, and men wearing raccoon
furs or trench coats clearly showing hip pocket flasks bulging
under them—with both sexes ready to break out in an im-
promptu Charleston at any given moment. Or so it seemed to
me.

All this sassy glamour was rather awe inspiring but I was
more awed by the evidence I saw that Washington College was
as intellectual as it was sophisticated. This evidence consisted
chiefly of the books Carolyn brought home—poems by Edna
St. Vincent Millay and the collected works of Joseph Conrad
and O. Henry, and others.

Millay was not a total stranger to me because her poem
about the pear tree was one of my mother's favorites, but this

thin book which Carolyn brought home showed another side to the poet which my mother did not know, or, if she did, chose not to mention. There was a strong mixture of gaiety and sadness in many of the poems; Millay seemed to be enjoying life but also seemed too much aware that the whole thing was not likely to last very long. I still cannot read her poem "What Lips My Lips Have Kissed" without getting goose pimples, particularly the lines which say "but the rain is full of ghosts tonight that tap and sigh upon the glass and listen for reply."

I read Millay's little book several times, but O. Henry's short stories gave me a much more extended source of delight; I read every story in all fourteen volumes. No one accused O. Henry of being an intellectual, even in those days, but he was the essence of sophistication in my eyes. He caused the slums of New York City to glow with a sparkling glamour which even Damon Runyon's Broadway guys and dolls of the 1920s could not equal. O. Henry found enchanting characters scattered all over the streets of his "Bagdad on the Subway," but the most appealing ones to me were Della and Jim in "The Gift of the Magi" and Hetty and Cecilia in "The Third Ingredient."

Just what Conrad said or did to convince me that the students and professors at Washington College were a noble lot during the early 1920s is unclear to me now. My most vivid recollections concern his roommate, Jeff Messick, and the college's two literary societies, the Adelphian and Mt. Vernon. Jeff, as Conrad always depicted him, was a bright, idealistic fellow with a sense of purpose and high integrity, but who also had a tart sense of humor which kept such a noble person from seeming dull. The Mt. Vernon and Adelphian literary socie-ties debated such subjects as "Resolved that the pen is mightier than the sword" or "Virtue is its own reward." These topics seem ridiculous now, but during the early 1920s Conrad's fellow students at Washington College debated them in all seriousness. Although the idealism of Conrad's college years and the sophistication of Carolyn's both had a strong influence on my opinion of Washington College, what impressed me most of all was the college's basketball team, the Flying Pentagon.

Before the Bridge

During the 1920s the sports pages of the nation were given over to colorful names for athletes and athletic organizations. There were the Four Horsemen of Notre Dame and the Galloping Ghost in football, the Sultan of Swat and the Big Train in baseball, the Manassa Mauler in boxing, and the Flying Pentagon in basketball.

Grantland Rice, whose sports column appeared regularly in the *Sun*, coined the phrase Four Horsemen when Notre Dame's most famous backfield ran roughshod over a great Army team in 1924. He also called Red Grange the Galloping Ghost when Illinois humiliated Michigan that same year. Damon Runyon called Jack Dempsey the Manassa Mauler when Dempsey mauled and battered such giants as Willard and Firpo into submission in a round or two for each. Who first called Babe Ruth the Sultan of Swat and Walter Johnson the Big Train I do not know, but Wilson, then writing sports for the *Sun*, gave Washington College's basketball team its name of Flying Pentagon, when it won six games on six successive nights on a whirlwind trip through Maryland, Virginia, and the District of Columbia during the winter of 1923.

This was Conrad's senior year in college and his letters home were filled with the magic of this fabulous team which earned its name during the single week but went on to win the state championship with a record of twenty-one victories against only two defeats. His most interesting letter told how the team had defeated Virginia Military Institute (VMI) and Washington and Lee University, both located in Lexington, Virginia, on successive nights. On Tuesday the Flying Pentagon (not yet given that name) defeated Washington and Lee while a group of VMI cadets cheered for the visitors. The next night an even larger and noisier group of Washington and Lee students went over to VMI to root for the visitors from Maryland, who obligingly won once more. By the end of the 1923 season the name of Flying Pentagon had become so entrenched in the life of Washington College that its top honor society was called the Silver Pentagon.

The 1924 Washington College basketball team was even

better than the 1923 outfit and went undefeated, again winning the state championship. It kept the name of Flying Pentagon and so did all succeeding basketball teams for the next two decades—until the teams became so weak and lost so frequently that Crawling Pentagon would have seemed more appropriate in describing them. But this collapse of basketball came several years after I had graduated, and in 1929 when I entered the college, the Flying Pentagon was still a name which conjured up visions of Mercury with wings on his heels.

In summary, I was convinced that I was entering a very special place indeed. I knew that it was the only college which had been expressly granted, by George Washington himself, the right to use Washington's name. So I thought that all other colleges, such as George Washington University, Washington and Jefferson, Washington and Lee, when they used George's name were imposters of a sort. I even believed that Washington College at Chestertown, Maryland, was the chief adornment which had ever been attached to the name of Washington, even though I was aware that one state, the nation's capital city, and one very tall monument had all been named in his honor. I did not know then that Washington also had thirty-two counties, four hundred cities and townships, ten lakes, and seven mountains named in his honor, but it would have made no difference if I had. I still would have regarded Washington College at Chestertown, Maryland, as his greatest honor.

Any student entering any college and harboring notions of the kind I had was inevitably doomed to suffer disillusionment. Mine began almost immediately—with the football season. Washington College lost every game on its schedule except one—a tie with American University.

But even worse than the long string of defeats was the fact that all newspapers published outside the state apparently felt that their readers had never heard of Washington College and did not know where it was located. The *Washington Star,* the *New York Herald-Tribune,* and the *Philadephia Inquirer,* for example, carried no stories about our football games but did list

Before the Bridge

the scores in the tabulations which they made each Sunday:

Swarthmore	13
Washington (Md.)	0
Albright	40
Washington (Md.)	0

It was that Md. in parentheses which was so galling because I noticed that when these papers listed the scores of Washington and Lee or Washington and Jefferson they never felt compelled to put Va. or Pa. after these colleges, just as they never put Mass. after Harvard or Conn. after Yale.

So far as I know, Roland E. "Reds" Bullock was the only one of my fellow students who was offended by this practice of the newspapers. At least Reds was the only one who ever said anything about it to me, but he and I discussed this sad state of affairs, off and on, for the last three years we were in college together.

Reds Bullock was a remarkable fellow for many reasons, one of which was that he barely managed to accumulate enough credits to receive a degree, but he was bright enough to have graduated summa cum laude. In fact, I believe he might have graduated with highest honors if the college schedule had been shifted either forward or backward by twelve hours.

Reds was what is now known as a night person. That is, he was wide awake during the hours of darkness but was either asleep or on the verge of sleep during most of the daylight hours. The result of this being out of phase with the scholastic program was that Reds either entirely missed attendance at most of his classes if they were scheduled during the period from 8:00 A.M. to noon, or if he got there he often fell asleep. The average college student would have flunked out in a year or less, following Red's program of class attendance and attention, and it was a great tribute to his native intellect that he managed to stick around until he graduated. Everyone liked him—even the professors in whose classes he slept so frequently.

Washington College and Bushrod

He usually slept quietly with his head slumped forward, but occasionally his head fell to one side or even slightly backward and on these occasions he would snore. One day in Dr. Howell's freshman economics class, which Reds took when he was a junior, he snored more loudly than usual, and Dr. Howell felt compelled to wake him up.

"Mr. Bullock, I appreciate the frankness of your remarks about how interesting my lecture is, but some of your classmates are trying to take notes and your snoring is interfering with their work. Either you will have to stay awake here in the classroom or go back to your own room and sleep more comfortably."

Reds grinned when he told me about this incident later but added, "If I go back to my own room, it just wakes me up. I can't sleep after 11:00 A.M." That really seemed to be his problem. He regularly became sleepy at between 3:00 and 4:00 A.M. and was widest awake from 6:00 P.M. to 2:00 A.M. the next day. I once asked him why he didn't stay up all night sometime, become very sleepy like the rest of us at 11:00 P.M., and thus get on the standard college schedule.

"I've tried it, and it doesn't work. Neither does it do me any good to try to sleep for twenty-four hours straight and get on schedule that way. I always wake up at 11:00 A.M. or noon. I think nature just intended me to work the night shift and sleep during the day shift."

Reds often managed to find some person who would stay up with him, playing cards or shooting the bull, until his own bedtime but most of the time he did not. Consequently, from about midnight until 3:00 A.M. he rather regularly did a lot of reading, but not necessarily books related to college courses. He was better educated than most college students—in the fields which interested him, such as history, biography, philosophy, and humor. His own lively puckish sense of humor was regularly evident whenever he talked on any subject. Most mortals had a foolish streak in them, as Reds saw it.

When he first mentioned to me that he had noticed how the newspaper sports columns nearly always wrote "Washington College (Md.)" when they gave the football scores, he had already arrived at a conclusion as to why they did it that way.

"The whole trouble, as I see it, lies in the fact that it apparently never occurred to the founders of this college that later on still other colleges might be named for George Washington. The later ones have all become distinctive; we now have George Washington University, Washington State University, Washington and Lee, Washington and Jefferson, and so on. And everyone knows where they are located, so when some reader sees plain Washington College he wonders if some identifying front or back name has been left off. So they add Maryland in parentheses. My home is only a hundred miles or so from here, in southern Pennsylvania, but when I go home for holidays people ask me why I decided to go all the way to the West Coast to find a college. Or they ask me how things are in the District of Columbia, and if I see President Hoover very often. We need a new name for this college— something distinctive which will identify it, maybe Washington and Lincoln College or Washington and Buchanan College. Nobody ever writes Virginia in parentheses after Washington and Lee."

I sensed that Reds was in one of his freewheeling moods. The slow grin which often wrinkled his face and gave emphasis to the difference between his very white skin and his reddish freckles was wider than usual when he leaned back on his bed and continued.

"Maybe we should call it Washington and Grant College. That way we would have the winner at Appomattox while all they have in Virginia is the loser. Or maybe we should call it Washington and Adams College, for the first two Presidents. Better still, we could call it Washington and John Quincy Adams College. That would certainly be distinctive enough so no one would wonder where it was located. Or how about Washington and Burr or Washington and Arnold College? Or Washington and Fillmore?"

Reds kept his soliloquy going for half an hour or so and during the course of it combined Washington with just about every name in American history. When I left him to go to bed myself, he had started to make a list of his proposals and said he would discuss it with me later.

"If we can agree on a new name we can take it up with the college authorities and maybe finally give Washington College a distinctive name."

However, he never said anything else to me on the subject all that year, and I forgot about it entirely until we were juniors. Then Reds hailed me one day: "How about Booker T. Washington College as a new name?"

We laughed about that suggestion for a few minutes and once again the subject of a new name for Washington College was dropped. I thought it was permanently disposed of, until about a week before we were due to graduate, I ran into Reds in the hall just outside Dr. Howell's office in William Smith Hall.

"I've got it—the perfect name. It is all in here," he went on, pointing to a small book which he held in his hand.

I must have looked blank because Reds began to explain what he was talking about.

"Let's call it Bushrod Washington College. That is a perfect new name for our alma mater. No one will ever wonder where Bushrod Washington College is."

I felt even blanker than I had felt before he began to explain.

"Why bushrod? What is bushrod?"

"Bushrod was a man. Not only that, he was a very distinguished man and a nephew of George Washington himself. It tells all about him in this little book called *The Washingtons of Virginia*. Bushrod Washington was a member of the first Supreme Court of the United States, a biographer of his Uncle George, and one of the founders of the Phi Beta Kappa honor society. He is a perfect candidate to have a college named after him."

Maybe the prospect of imminent graduation had given me a light-headed outlook on things, but it suddenly seemed to me that Reds had come up with a great idea.

"That's a marvelous suggestion, Reds. What are we going to do about it?"

"Let's take it up with the college authorities. Dr. Howell is Registrar of the College so let's start with him."

Whereupon we barged into Dr. Howell's office and found him standing behind his desk with a set of golf clubs leaning against the desk.

"What can I do for you, boys?" he asked.

"We have a new name for Washington College," Reds replied.

Dr. Howell sat down in his chair.

"What name and why?"

Reds had taken over the job as spokesman for the two of us since it was his idea even though I was enthusiastically behind it.

"We want to name it Bushrod Washington College."

"Just because Bushrod was George's nephew?"

"No; because if I tell people back home I went to Bushrod Washington College, they will quit asking me where the college is."

Dr. Howell broke into a wide grin.

"I think you have a great idea, boys. I'll bring up your recommendation at the next meeting of the Board of Visitors and Governors. Now I have to get moving. I have a golf date in half an hour."

Many good politicians and psychologists know that sometimes the best way to dispose of an idiotic idea is to appear to go along with it for a while, and I suspect that Dr. Howell simply gave us that treatment. Anyway, that early June day in 1933 was the first and last time I ever heard anyone mention Bushrod Washington College.

SEVEN

First By-Line

IN his book, *Newspaper Days,* H. L. Mencken described how excited he was when, as an apprentice reporter for the *Baltimore Herald,* the first two brief pieces he ever wrote for publication actually appeared in print. One of the stories was a two-sentence account of the theft of a horse and buggy and the other was a one-sentence report on a cinematograph exhibition at a Baltimore church. There was not the slightest thing remarkable about either story but to young Mencken they were magic.

I was up with the milkman the next morning to search the paper and when I found both of my pieces, exactly as written, there ran such thrills through my system as a barrel of brandy and 100,000 volts of electricity could not have matched.

Mencken was a man apart among mere mortals, and I cannot remember ever encountering any stimulant which matched his barrel of brandy and 100,000 volts, but two things did happen to me during my freshman year at Washington College which gave me an idea how Mencken felt that morning. Both of them gave me an awakening jolt similar to what I felt when I once grabbed the business end of a spark coil on a Model-T Ford.

One of these eye-opening events was the arrival of the first check I ever received in payment for something I had written for publication, and the other was the first time I ever saw my name written above a story in a newspaper.

Before the Bridge

The check was from the *Baltimore Sun* for sports items I had submitted during the month of October 1929, and it arrived only a few days after the stock market crash that year. It should, however, be noted that this disturbing event had no significance to me, and I was only vaguely aware that it had occurred since I seldom read anything in the newspaper in those days except the sports pages. No one in my family except Wilson owned any stocks and his holdings consisted of only a few shares of Standard Oil of New Jersey and the Pennsylvania Railroad. But cash was something I did think about a lot since I seldom had any of it, and the *Sun*'s check was for a few cents more than twelve dollars—a really magnificent sum in view of how easy to come by it all seemed to me.

I should report at once that as a sixteen-year-old college freshman, I had neither the confidence nor the experience required to establish a profitable relationship with the *Sun*. Wilson had handled this crucial matter when I visited him in Baltimore early in October. He took me down to the Sun Building, showed me the linotype machines and printing presses in action, and introduced me to several people in the sports department where he worked. The only man I remember clearly was C. M. Gibbs whose sports column, called "Gibberish," I had read with delight for several years. However, the really important man I met that day was a copyreader who had the duty of setting up some of the sports pages each day. His first name was Andy but his last name has escaped me; it may have been Watson, Wason, Watkins, or something close to those sounds.

Anyway, Wilson told me that he had arranged with Andy to have me submit brief sports items concerning Washington College athletics, which could be used as fillers when more important stories did not fill up the entire page. Andy told me the *Sun* would pay three cents a line for anything he used from what I sent him.

Later, Wilson gave me some detailed instructions as to how my stories should be written and submitted.

64

First By-Line

Don't make any attempts to write great literature. It would probably astonish Andy if you did, and he wouldn't be able to use such material because sports fans want what they read to be simple and similar to what they have been used to reading. They want to read clichés and other things which are familiar to them. You have been reading the kind of things they like in the *Sun* for several years now. Sports fans can stand a few new ideas from time to time but such stuff had better not appear too frequently or else it starts to make them itch, scratch themselves, and look for another paper.

They can stand a few quotations from literature but if a quotation appears it should be one of the better known ones or else the reader will think the whole thing is gibberish. And don't try any poetry of the kind I sometimes put at the top of my column because poetry simply won't fly on the sports pages except in a signed column, and none of your items will be signed even if Andy uses them. Also, you shouldn't send him too much stuff during the football season because Washington College football teams win only about one game a season, and if this team starts getting a lot of publicity people will begin to wonder why this is so. You should be able to do a lot better during the basketball season. You usually shouldn't send in more than three pieces a week, unless the coach shoots one of the players or some such thing, and you should break each piece into paragraphs which can stand alone so Andy can use one, two, or three of them, as his needs to fill out a page occur. Also, it will help to include a few names in each story. Refer to something Coach Kibler or the team captain has done in preparation for the next game, or if one of the regulars has pulled a muscle in his leg, tell who he is and who will start in his place.

"Finally," he told me,

If you expect the piece to be used in Friday's paper, you have to get it in the mail on Wednesday so Andy will receive it on Thursday. And it should be typed because your handwriting is awful, and he won't have time to decode it.

I had no typewriter and could not use one anyway but one of my classmates in West Hall had one and regularly typed his class assignments. This accomplished fellow was named J. Milton Noble. He hailed from Denton, Maryland, and readily agreed to do my typing for twelve cents per page. It cost two cents for a stamp in those days, and so I had at least fourteen cents invested in every story I mailed to the *Sun*, but since I usually had enough material for fifty or sixty lines in each communiqué, there was room for a clear profit of well over a dollar if Andy used all of what I sent him.

Milton seemed to enjoy his part in my literary efforts, after the first piece appeared exactly as we had submitted it. He had been somewhat skeptical about the whole affair when I first approached him and seemed inclined to think I had just dreamed up the idea of writing for the *Sun*.

I must have followed Wilson's advice pretty effectively because nearly everything I submitted was used with little or no revision. Sometimes a paragraph or two was included in a summary of football games scheduled for the coming weekend, but more often than not the story appeared under its own headline. All told, during October the *Sun* must have used about four hundred lines because, as already mentioned, they sent me a check for about twelve dollars.

The first item which appeared gave me quite a thrill but it would have been a much bigger one if it had been generally known around the campus that I had written the piece. As it was, only Noble and I knew who the author was, and even after we began to tell others most of the students remained in ignorance because we were only freshmen without any wide circle of friends. Milton did a better job of publicizing my literary efforts than I did because I was somewhat inhibited by the necessity of maintaining a pretense of modesty.

However, by the end of October Washington College's football team had received about three times as much space in the *Sun* as it had been accustomed to, and the names of Coach

First By-Line

Tom Kibler and Captain William J. "Red" Burk had appeared several times in my dispatches because they represented my best opportunity to follow Wilson's advice about using names as much as possible. And this soon had very pleasant consequences for me.

Wilson had told me that it was in order, from time to time, to quote statements by some of the people I wrote about.

> It isn't necessary to say exactly what they said. In fact, it is usually necessary to dress up what an athlete says in one way or another. There are a few exceptions, but most athletes, particularly professional ones, can't speak without loading up their speech with double negatives and four-letter words. College athletes are somewhat different but not too much. So if you quote one and it comes out making sense he won't mind, and Andy will appreciate having it arrive that way on his desk.

So I quoted Captain Red Burk a couple of times without ever having spoken to him at all. The second time this happened he came to West Hall to see me. This was a great honor in itself, because Red Burk was a really big man on the campus. He was not only captain of the football team but was also shortstop on the baseball team, president of his fraternity, and editor-in-chief of the college newspaper, *The Collegian*.
"Hey, kid," he said when he stuck his head in my door, "are you Wingate?"

I said I was and he then asked if I had written the story in the *Sun* that morning. I admitted that too, with a little trepidation that he might say I had no right to quote him without speaking to him first.

But he didn't. Instead he grinned in a friendly manner and said: "Nice going. How would you like to write some pieces for the college newspaper?"

I said that would suit me fine and from then on, for the rest of my college days I wrote for the *Collegian* or the *Elm*, which was the name the college paper used after 1931. I served the *Elm* in various capacities, including that of editor-in-chief during my senior year, but nothing I did for the *Elm* gave me quite the electric thrill which went through my system when the final issue of the 1930 *Collegian* came out.

However, before that issue was printed I did a lot of writing for the *Sun*. The baskeball season was, as Wilson had predicted, a relative bonanza for me, and Andy printed more of my stuff during January of 1930 than in any other two months combined. My February check was for exactly thirty-one dollars, as I recall it, reflecting the fact that the 1929-1930 version of Washington College's Flying Pentagon was still something to excite sports fans. The captain of the basketball team that year was a really fine athlete named Stanley "Gerry" Giraitis who was written up in Ripley's *Believe It or Not!* when he scored five field goals in fifty-nine seconds of play. This would be no easy feat even in today's style of run-and-gun basketball, but in 1930 it was phenomenal since most teams scored less than thirty points in an entire game.

All told, I wrote about three thousand lines for the *Sun's* sports pages that year and received nearly ninety dollars for my efforts. Since I spent a total of less than a hundred hours in all this writing, I was paid at the incredible rate of about a dollar an hour, whereas the most I had ever received for any other kind of work was about a fourth of that rate.

It would be a dreadful chore to dig out and identify everything I wrote for the *Sun* because they also had a regular Chestertown correspondent who occasionally sent them sports stories. But if I did the search, I am convinced I would find that I had faithfully followed Wilson's instructions—that is to say, I made generous use of the best known clichés and never offered up a single new thought of any kind or even a new way of expressing an old thought.

In my writing for the college newspaper I felt I had a freer hand and some of the gaudier pieces which appeared in it during the spring of 1930 were mine. They reflected my attempts to show that I was another Grantland Rice in the making. However, I can't prove that all of the purple prose in the sports section of the *Collegian* was mine since others wrote some stuff which was just as gaudy. And practically none of it was signed except a few pieces by editor-in-chief Red Burk himself.

It apparently was a policy of editor-in-chief Burk not to identify the authors of the stories in the *Collegian* and this was a source of disappointment to me. However, I was only a freshman and continued to write all the stories assigned to me. I was particularly pleased when Burk asked me to write up the final home athletic event of the spring of 1930. This was a baseball game between Washington College and Mount St. Mary's College for the collegiate state championship of Maryland.

Washington College had good baseball teams during the 1920s, even though their baseball teams did not rank as high as their basketball teams, but Mount St. Mary's had the best record of all Maryland colleges in the spring of 1930. In addition, the Mounties, as they were called, had a shortstop who was so good that big league scouts had been following him around for a couple of months. This marvel was a fellow named Carrigan, and I looked forward to seeing him play.

Carrigan played well that day but Red Burk, playing at the same shortstop position, played even better, and Washington College won the game. Burk ran out from under his hat several times and his flaming red hair seemed to be everywhere between second base and third whenever the Mounties were at bat. Inspired by all this red hair and freed from the restraints Wilson and Andy had put upon me in my dispatches to the *Sun* I ran wild in my account of the game for the *Collegian.*

I spent two hours after the game writing my account. When I turned the story in at about five o'clock, I was proud of it. I said that the entire Washington College team had played heroically but the brightest star of them all had been Red Burk. I gave the impression that even Honus Wagner had never played a better game at shortstop and said flatly that Burk had outplayed his more highly touted rival, the illustrious big league prospect Carrigan. Finally I said that not even Glen Wright could have done a better job than Red Burk did.

Glen Wright? That name needs an explanation now, but it

69

did not in 1930 for anyone following baseball. Glen Wright was generally regarded as the best fielding shortstop in the big leagues at that time and in addition was batting at about three hundred and fifty while most shortstops were lucky to hit two hundred and fifty.

The final issue of the *Collegian* was being held up to permit coverage of this ball game, and it appeared promptly the next day. I could hardly wait to see it because I hoped that Red Burk would give my story a featured position in his paper. But Red exceeded my fondest hopes because my story appeared in the top right-hand column of the front page.

Not only that, but it carried a by-line. The author was given as Philip V. Wingate. It would have taken at least a full jigger of 90 proof bourbon whiskey and a jolt from a 24-volt telephone battery to equal the thrill I felt when I saw my very first by-line in print. True enough, Red had omitted one "l" in my first name and had replaced my middle initial "J." with a "V." but a by-line is a by-line, and there was no one else at Washington College, except me, with a name anything like that in the by-line.

I was so pleased with the whole business that I sent a copy of the front page of the *Collegian* to Wilson and told him that the editor had been doubly kind to me—first by putting my story on the front page and second by giving me a by-line. Wilson did not reply to my letter, but the next time I saw him, he immediately said to me: "Your editor wasn't being kind to you at all. You left the son-of-a-gun no choice. If he hadn't put your name above the story all his friends would have been sure Red Burk wrote the story himself."

EIGHT

Lacrosse Chief

MOST authorities in the field including George Catlin and Jean de Brebeuf, agree that before the time of Columbus the American Indians were playing some version of lacrosse from Canada to Florida and as far west as the Great Plains. However, except for one undocumented statement by Maryland historian Matthew Page Andrews there is nothing in the record to show that the Indians living along the Chesapeake Bay ever engaged in the sport. Andrews said that the warlike Wicomico Indians on the Eastern Shore of Maryland may have played lacrosse, but he never documented this suggestion.

It is, nevertheless, an unquestionable fact that white man lacrosse has flourished more verdantly along the shores of the Chesapeake Bay than in any other part of the United States. Maryland has been the generally recognized center of lacrosse for about a century now. Since Johns Hopkins University won its first national championship in 1881, Maryland colleges have tended to dominate the sport. Four of them—Johns Hopkins, University of Maryland, the U. S. Naval Academy, and St. John's College at Annapolis—have all won two or more national collegiate lacrosse championships. Hopkins, alone, has won more national titles than all out-of-state colleges combined although schools from New Jersey, New York, Virginia, North Carolina, and Massachusetts have won one or more national championships.

During the fifty-year period from 1875 to 1925 lacrosse was so popular in Baltimore that it became as closely identified with the city as crab cakes, Francis Scott Key, Babe Ruth, and H. L. Mencken. Nevertheless, during all this time lacrosse remained as foreign to the Eastern Shore of Maryland as cricket or Irish hurling. Very few Eastern Shoremen had ever seen a game and many had never heard of it. This situation began to change in 1928 when William P. "Chief" Beatty introduced the sport at Washington College, and today lacrosse fans from Chestertown to Salisbury watch both high school and college lacrosse with as much enthusiasm as the most avid fans in Baltimore, Annapolis, and College Park.

The development of lacrosse on the western shore of the Chesapeake came before my time, and I learned about it only after Wilson wrote a series of articles for the *Baltimore Sun* on the history and origin of the game. However, I watched the growth of lacrosse on the Eastern Shore from a seat so far up front that I even got up on the stage and played a small role in the show myself. My part as a bit player in the drama of Eastern Shore lacrosse started under the direction of the aforementioned Chief Beatty.

Just how or when Coach Beatty got the name of Chief I never learned but everyone called him that. It may be that he had some Indian blood in him because he had the typical high cheek bones of the Indian and he was a magnificent physical specimen who looked somewhat like Jack Dempsey, who was part Indian. Chief was a little over six feet tall and weighed about one hundred and ninety-five pounds. Athletes his size usually played defense but he had been a close attack man and must have been a formidable assignment for any defense player in 1926 when he won first team All-American honors.

While Chief was a great lacrosse player he had come to Washington College as an assistant coach of football because he also had been a star player on several of Curley Byrd's football teams which had started to attract national attention by knocking off Yale and other football powers of that era. In addition to serving as assistant coach of football, Chief taught a class in freshman English, as a part of his contract with the college. Starting a lacrosse team was his own idea and he was able to talk the college authorities into it in the spring of 1929 after the Johns Hopkins team of 1928 had attracted so much

Lacrosse Chief

favorable attention by participating in the Olympic Games in Amsterdam that year.

I first met Chief in the fall of 1929, but I had little contact with him during the first half of that scholastic year since I was not a football player and had not been assigned to his freshman English class, which was for those who had not scored well in grammar on the placement tests for freshmen. I don't believe I wrote anything at all about him in my dispatches to the *Sun* during the football season. However, a classmate, Warren Johnson, was both a football player and a member of Chief's English class, and Warren was full of stories about Chief and the way he taught English to his class.

This class spent the first full month parsing a single sentence which became indelibly fixed in Warren's mind. The sentence read: "A man with a bowler hat was seen spitting on the street." But according to Warren when Chief read the sentence, it came out: "A man wid a bowler hat was seen spitting on de street." Whether Chief or someone else decided that this sentence was uniquely suited to the teaching of English to those short on grammar I do not know. I do know that Warren thought the Chief's English class was a complete waste of time. And perhaps it was, but Warren was not quite right in saying that Chief pronounced "with" as "wid" and "the" as "de". He was close but a little wide of the mark. Actually, Chief had one of the most remarkable accents I have ever heard. It seemed to be made up of about equal parts of South Baltimore, Boston, and Hoboken, New Jersey. The closest to it that I can recall was the accent of Theodore R. McKeldin who served several terms as Mayor of Baltimore and Governor of Maryland. The main difference between the two accents was that McKeldin had eliminated any suggestion of "de" when he wanted to say "the."

It would be highly misleading to give the impression that chief was a big dumb athletic jock who had learned nothing except football and lacrosse during his four years at the University of Maryland. He was an intelligent fellow and well educated in fields which interested him. I remember the day

7 3

he demonstrated to his lacrosse players how to cradle the stick above his head and change from a right-handed throwing stance to a left-handed one, all in one smooth easy motion.

"When you get that down pat, boys, you will be rolling in ever-flowering meads of asphodel."

I knew he was quoting from something when he said that, but it was a year later before I learned that Chief was giving us a quotation from Pope's translation of the Odyssey.

My fondest ambition, when I entered college, was to earn a varsity letter and strut around the campus and town with a big black W on my chest. If I had been given the choice of only one item from a group of three consisting of a varsity letter, a summa cum laude degree, or a Nobel prize, I would have chosen the first, provided only that it carried as much money as the Nobel prize. I had never played football or basketball in high school, since we had no team in these sports, and so I assumed that my letter would have to be earned in baseball. However, I often worried that I would not be good enough to make the baseball team since Coach Kibler always had a strong team in this sport. I was a third baseman, and I knew that Kibler's third baseman a few years back had been Jake Flowers who later went on to star with the St. Louis Cardinals in World Series competition.

Nevertheless, in spite of all fears and doubts I was resolved to be a third baseman. So when Chief issued his call for lacrosse players early in March of 1930, I ignored it. In another few weeks the snow and slush would be gone, and baseball practice would start.

Although I was not among them that first day, the lacrosse players were an arresting sight arrayed in their long white pants and sweatshirts, and I went down to the south end of the campus to watch them work out. Fascinated by the skirmishes for loose balls, I began to think that lacrosse had possibilities when I learned that it was perfectly legal to knock your opponent out of the way or the stick out of his hand before trying to scoop up the ball in your own crab net.

When that first practice was over, Chief sent his squad on a race around the still partly frozen campus which had a dirty

Lacrosse Chief

rind of snow left over from the last snow of the winter. At the end of this race the panting warriors charged into the gym waving their sticks like so many braves on the warpath, and I followed them. The clatter of their cleats on the concrete and their jostling, yelling, and good-humored swearing in the showers all made for good comradery, and lacrosse suddenly seemed to me to be a great sport.

Also, I had noticed that during first practice several of Chief's warriors seemed to know as little about the game as I did. When they tried to throw the ball, it dribbled off the end of their sticks, and when they tried to pick up a loose ball, it seemed as elusive as a drop of quicksilver.

The next day I decided to become a lacrosse player and accordingly presented myself to Chief in his office. He was smoking a big black cigar and did not seem to be excited by the late appearance of his newest lacrosse player.

"Kid," he said, glancing up and down my one hundred thirty pounds spread over six feet, "I gave out all the uniforms yesterday, but I'll let you have a stick, and you can practice in your gym clothes."

So my lacrosse career began without gloves, helmet, or uniform, and throughout the 1930 season I remained the scrubbiest of scrubs. I never had a uniform until shortly before the last game of the season when another scrub decided to give the game back to the Indians and turned in his uniform.

The highlight of Washington College's 1930 lacrosse season was a game with a touring group of all-stars from Oxford and Cambridge universities in England. There were nine Rhodes scholars in the Oxford-Cambridge group, including two former All-Americans from the United States—Larkin Farinholt of Johns Hopkins and Al Cormsweet from Brown University. The British were a powerful outfit and beat most of the good American college teams they played during their month-long tour.

Why they wanted to play Washington College, in only its second season of lacrosse, I never learned. The idea probably originated with Chief who was highly enthusiastic about playing the visitors from England. They asked for a payment of

Before the Bridge

three hundred dollars to cover their travel expenses to the Eastern Shore, and Chief appeared before an assembly of the student body to ask that this payment be authorized since it was not in the athletic department's budget. One dollar added to each student activity fee for the year would do the job, he said.

"Think what an honor it would be for us to beat Oxford University, where they have been playing lacrosse for fifty years, while this is only our second year. Not only that, but I hear that one of their players is a titled nobleman and very charming." Whereupon, Chief held up his right hand, with the little finger daintily curved, and sipped from an imaginary cup of tea. The students voted unanimously, as I recall it, to have the three hundred dollars added to our charges for the year. After all, our parents would not be expected to pay much attention to just one more dollar of school expenses.

Wilson fell into the spirit of the occasion and wrote that the upcoming lacrosse game between Oxford-Cambridge and Washington College would represent the first hand-to-hand combat between the British and Eastern Shoremen since the Kent County militia had killed Sir Peter Parker at the battle of Caulk's Field during the war of 1812. He also told me privately that if Washington College won the game it would be the biggest upset since Andrew Jackson beat the British at New Orleans.

Sadly, it turned out that the British had learned some things since Caulk's Field and New Orleans, or perhaps it was that Chief's warriors were not as competent as Andrew Jackson's had been. Oxford-Cambridge beat us by a score of 18 to 0, on a soggy field during a cold steady rain. It was awful, and even the tea held at Reid Hall to give the coeds a chance to meet the British did little or nothing to lift the spirits of the student body. As for me, I stood on the sidelines throughout the game, holding my stick but without a uniform or helmet, and was not even invited to the tea.

However, as already mentioned, a substitute quit the squad late in May and I inherited his uniform and began to get in an

Lacrosse Chief

occasional scrimmage against the varsity. During the last week of the season Chief had his friend and former teammate from College Park, Harry Wilson, come over to Chestertown to help with the coaching. The squad was split into two groups with Harry Wilson being captain of one and Chief the other. I was on Chief's team and at one point was racing up the sidelines, cradling my stick with the ball in it, when Harry cut me down with a clean body block. My helmet, which had no strap on it, went one way and I went another, but by some miracle I held on to my stick and flipped the ball to a teammate as I was going down.

Chief helped me to my feet and erased all my pains with a brief comment: "Nice going, Kid, you are beginning to get the hang of it." The exhilaration which this remark created was mild compared to the thrill I felt when Chief fell in beside me on the way to gym after practice ended.

"You are coming along fine, Kid. I won't be back next year but a friend of mine, Gus Carothers, from Maryland will coach lacrosse, and he has asked me to give him a list of good prospects for next year. I'll put your name on the list."

We walked another forty yards or so together along the cinder track, and I could hear his cleats crunching cinders all the way but mine never touched those cinders. I was a foot or two above them, every step of the way, with my eyes fixed on that big black W which I could see in the distance.

Chief liked to call himself the Father of White Man Lacrosse on the Eastern Shore, a name first given to him by Wilson. And if he had heard it, he would have liked the explanation which Wilson brought back from the 1932 Olympic Games, as to why lacrosse had prospered so much along the shores of the Chesapeake Bay. Lacrosse, Wilson said, was an intellectual game.

Johns Hopkins had, for the second time, represented the United States in Olympic competition and Wilson had gone to Los Angeles to report on the games in general, and on lacrosse in particular, just as he had done in 1928 at the Amsterdam Olympics. But this time he was working for the *Baltimore News*

77

because William Randolph Hearst had lured him from the *Sun* by the simple device of offering him exactly twice what the *Sun* had been paying him.

Working with Louella Parsons, Hollywood columnist for Hearst, Wilson arranged to have Will Rogers serve as announcer for a lacrosse game between Hopkins and a Canadian team. Rogers was proud of the fact that he was part Cherokee Indian and he kept a huge crowd of about seventy thousand, the largest ever to see a lacrosse game, in a good humor by his remarks.

"People sometimes ask me if my people came over on the *Mayflower*. I tell them 'no but they met the boat.' That is, they would have met the boat but they got so excited watching a lacrosse game between the Cherokees and Algonquins that they forgot the *Mayflower* was due to dock at Plymouth Rock that day."

Later on when Pete Reynolds, playing defense for Hopkins, flattened a Canadian attack man in front of the Hopkins goal, Rogers chuckled with delight and said: "Folks, lacrosse looks like a real intellectual game to me. I expect to see somebody's brains knocked out any minute now."

Wilson enjoyed himself repeating all this to me late in 1932 and said:

I believe Will Rogers may have explained why lacrosse is so popular in Maryland. It is an intellectual game. Look at who the great coaches of lacrosse in Maryland have been. Dinty Moore, who coached St. John's to two national championships, was President of the Maryland College for Women and Dr. Ray Van Orman and Dr. Kelso Morrill have coached Hopkins to two Olympic championships while Dr. Reginald Truitt and Dr. Jack Faber have made the University of Maryland's teams good enough to play anyone on even terms. Apparently you need to have a doctor's degree to be a good coach of lacrosse.

I found the notion that lacrosse was an intellectual game to be very appealing and said so. Since I had already received that

Lacrosse Chief

much coveted varsity letter in 1932 and had been elected captain of the Washington College lacrosse team for 1933, I was glad to hear anything which puffed up lacrosse. All this, plus the notion that lacrosse was for intellectuals, probably caused both my head and chest to swell a bit, and Wilson may have noticed these swellings. Anyway he promptly gave me an antidote for both ailments.

"On the other hand, some people claim that you can take almost any ordinary athlete, beat his brains out with a stick, and make a good lacrosse player out of what is left."

I have seen most of the good lacrosse players during the past fifty years, including invaders from Canada, England, and Australia, and they were a varied lot. Some were bright, others stupid, some big and some little, some short and some tall. But not one of them ever looked as tall to me as Chief Beatty seemed that day in 1930 when he walked along the cinder track, and I walked on air beside him.

NINE

Corn Borers and Bloomer Girls

ALTHOUGH I had traveled up and down both shores of the Chesapeake many times by the time I was eighteen years old, I had never been outside the boundaries of what the *Baltimore Sun* and H. L. Mencken called the Free State of Maryland. This insularity in my education ended abruptly when Wilson got summer jobs for Vic and me after we finished our second year of college.

These summer jobs took us into four new states—New Jersey, Pennsylvania, New York, and Connecticut—and during eight weeks I learned how to hunt the wild corn borer in his native habitat and a variety of other things including a secret concerning the Bloomer Girls Baseball Team, a now long defunct organization which was nationally famous during the early 1900s.

The year was 1931, the Great Depression was already two years old, and since unemployment was high all over the country Vic and I would have welcomed any kind of summer job. Therefore, the one Wilson got for us through U. S. Senator Phillips Lee Goldsborough seemed like manna from heaven. We became corn borer inspectors for the U. S. Department of Agriculture, at the princely salary of twenty-eight dollars per week, a sum which many families of five would have been delighted to have in those days.

Although soon to be thrown out of office, the Republicans still controlled the federal bureaucracy and Wilson told us that a letter from Senator Goldsborough was all we needed to obtain summer work for students. He was right. Whether the senator was simply repaying my father for past political help or was hoping to obtain some favorable publicity in the *Balti-*

Corn Borers and Bloomer Girls

more News-Post where Wilson was then writing both politics and football I do not know, but in any event we got the jobs.

We were instructed to report to Freehold, New Jersey, for a week of training before being assigned to the field, and we found it to be a charming little town about the size of Cambridge, located near the center of Monmouth County, about thirty miles east of Trenton. We arrived on a Sunday and located a rooming house, costing only fifty cents per person per night, right next to the firehouse. We went to bed that night feeling we had found a bargain since the room was neat, clean, and airy. However, the notion that we had found a bargain vanished about three o'clock in the morning when we were flung out of bed by the loudest clanging bell I have ever heard.

The town of Freehold in those days did not have a fire siren; instead it had a large bell mounted on top of the firehouse, about twenty feet from our open window, and when the fire chief wanted to summon his crew he pounded on this bell with a large hammer. The clang which resulted could be heard all over town, but in our room it was more than mere sound. The vibration rattled our windows, shook the floor, and caused the bed to do an Irish jig around the room. Nevertheless, after we learned from the landlady what was going on, we went back to bed, fell asleep in a few minutes, and were well rested when we reported for our first day of training as corn borer inspectors.

About sixty trainees assembled in the barn of a farmer located on the outskirts of Freehold, which apparently had been selected as a training area because the farmers in Monmouth County specialized in growing sweet corn for the New York City market and so had cornfields in a more advanced stage than was the case for areas growing corn for animal feed. While most of the trainees were students, many others were not. I remember a man named Zimmerman, with a heavy German accent, who said he was sixty-two years old and another middle-aged man who had been a cashier in an Ohio bank until his bank failed costing him both his job and his life savings which he had loyally deposited in the bank. Altogether we were a motley crew with probably only one thing in common; we were all Republicans or had Republican friends.

The training team was a well-organized one with a general director and six assistants who later became regional supervisors when we were dispersed to the field. The director opened the first training session by telling us that the corn borer was an insect which had recently been imported from Europe in a shipment of Hungarian broom corn and in a few years had shown that it was certain to be a threat to the entire American corn industry. So far, he said, it had been restricted to the northeastern part of the United States where it was already doing great damage to both field corn and sweet corn. The insect did its damage in the larval or worm stage attacking mostly the area of a cornstalk above the ear. These corn borer worms had voracious appetites, he said, and even a few of them might weaken a stalk so much that the tassel would fall off. Fortunately, he continued, the borer did not fly far in its winged stage, and one county might be heavily infested while a nearby area would be free of borers unless a shipment of corn should be received from an infested area. Our job, he told us, was to determine just where the European corn borer was so that the Department of Agriculture could quarantine these areas.

I had never seen a corn borer and was glad when someone asked what they looked like. The director then pulled a small bottle from his pocket and said that in it was a corn borer pickled in formaldehyde. He passed it around for all to inspect and in the bottle we saw a small white worm about half an inch long. It was about half as big as the corn ear worms which were quite familiar to me. We would see live corn borers in the fields around us, the director said, because the area was known to be badly infested.

We then broke up into groups and the various assistant directors led us into the fields. Our instructor said the way to find corn borers was to look for frass. This was a new term to all of us in the group, but it soon became a much used word because we learned that frass referred to worm droppings.

Corn Borers and Bloomer Girls

Quickly, we began to use it for the solid excrement of all forms of animal life including worms, birds, dogs, and horses.

"Watch out for the horse frass" was a common warning whenever we approached the barn on a new farm. Corn borer frass actually looked something like fine sawdust, and soon all of us could identify it when we found it clinging to the cornstalk. Then by breaking open the stalk we could usually find the corn borer itself still busily chewing away on the soft interior of the stalk.

When the training week was over, Vic and I were made a team, given a small pick-up truck and told to go to Bucks County, Pennsylvania, and make our headquarters at Morrisville, a small town just across the Delaware River from Trenton. It turned out to be a very happy location for us.

We ran out of money altogether on our third day in Morrisville because we had squandered some of the fifteen dollars we each started out with on such frivolities as movies and a couple of games of pool so we had barely enough left to pay the first week's room rent on a room we found in Morrisville. This room cost more than the one in Freehold, but it lacked the alarm bell which made the one in Freehold the most memorable one I ever slept in. We had been eating, during those first three days, at a small restaurant run by a Greek named George Christopolus, and we decided to ask George for credit until our first paycheck arrived the following week.

George agreed immediately, and from then on we ate with as much abandon as a hungry corn borer, and got to know much about our host. He was a bachelor who had no remaining relatives, either in this country or back in Greece, and he had taken out two life insurance policies—one payable to the State of Pennsylvania for twenty thousand dollars and the other to the United States for thirty thousand dollars—huge sums it seemed to me. George said his father had died a few years ago back in Greece at 105 years of age. "He drink a whole bottle of wine one night," George said. "He go to bed. He no wake up in the morning."

George's restaurant was located on the main highway

which passed through Morrisville, and he frequently had vagrants stop in his place to ask for a handout. He never refused them.

"Time is hard, and I no can turn away a hongry man so I offer them all some bread and water. If they no eat bread then they no hongry."

George was probably the hardest working man I ever met. He was the entire work force for his restaurant. Cook, waiter, janitor, and purchasing agent. He opened shop at 6:00 A.M., closed at 10:00 P.M., and slept in the single room above his restaurant. After we got to know him well, Vic and I asked him why he had trusted us that first week when we ran out of money.

"Because you look like honest boy," he said to Vic who had asked the question, "and also because you got that truck with the license tag which say U.S.D.A., and I no think the U. S. Government going to steal from me."

We never saw George again after we were transferred from Morrisville. I visited there in 1938, but since both George's restaurant and his building were gone, I don't know whether Pennsylvania and the United States had collected on their insurance policies or not. If George had a longevity equal to that of his wine-drinking father, they may still be waiting to collect.

After we received our first paycheck, Vic and I went to a street carnival in Morrisville and there met two pretty high school girls, Helen Wickham, a blonde, and Mildred Brown, a brunette, whom we frequently took to the movies in Trenton during the next four weeks. There was a movie house in Morrisville but it was a rather drab place which showed only old movies. However, the largest movie house in Trenton was a magnificent affair patterned after the Roxy in New York. It not only ran the top-line talkies but also had a vaudeville supplement. In the vaudeville shows they had live chorus girls every week, and on separate occasions movie stars Lon Chaney and Conrad Nagel were featured in these vaudeville parts. Tap dancer Bill Robinson was also scheduled to appear, but we

Corn Borers and Bloomer Girls

missed him because he arrived after we left town. Altogether, I suspect that Vic and I squandered a total of fifteen or twenty dollars on streetcar fare and movie tickets, trying to please and impress those two charming little gold diggers, Helen and Mildred.

In the meantime, we were busy during work hours trying to prove the presence of corn borers in Bucks County and in the third week we succeeded. When our supervisor, a man named Turner, came to visit us that week, we showed him some live corn borers which we had collected, and he agreed they were authentic borers and not just undersized ear worms. "However," he said, "I'll have to ship them to the Department's entomologists for final confirmation."

We also asked Turner what the Department of Agriculture would do about it then but he refused at first to tell us. When we pressed him, he finally grinned and said: "They will stick a pin with a red top on it in the map of Pennsylvania showing that Bucks County has corn borers and that will be the end of that."

We never received any direct word from Washington, but I guess they confirmed our findings because a week later we were transferred to Schenectady, New York. We left Morrisville with real regret because we liked both the town and its people—particularly Helen, Mildred, and our trusting Greek friend, George Christopolus.

When we moved to Schenectady, we actually roomed in Scotia, across the Mohawk River, but these two places did not compare with Trenton and Morrisville. In fact, the only happy memory I have about our second assignment is the fact that we found a movie house in Schenectady which regularly showed double features for a dime—if tickets were purchased before 6:00 P.M. Vic and I always made it on time and once saw James Cagney and Edward G. Robinson in a double feature on gangsters.

We never found any corn borers in the fields on either side of the Mohawk River and after two weeks of futile searching we were given our final transfer—to Winsted, Connecticut.

Before the Bridge

Winsted was in the northwest corner of the state and located on a bend of the Mad River which got its name, we were told, from the fact that it sometimes flooded badly during the spring rainy season. The Mad River was on its good behavior while we were in Winsted, but the town had suffered many blows from the depression. Clearly the town had once been a very attractive one with grassy lawns which were still well kept, but because unemployment was extremely high in Winsted, most of the stores and shops were either closed entirely or were just barely hanging on. The one movie house in town showed only silent movies and was open only on Friday and Saturday nights.

The only thing which kept Winsted from being a complete washout, so far as Vic and I were concerned, was the fact that the Bloomer Girls baseball team was scheduled to play an exhibition game against the Winsted All-Stars on the Saturday following our arrival on Sunday.

The word "bloomers" has just about vanished from the English language, but during the 1920s everyone knew that bloomers were a loose undergarment worn by women. This undergarment got its name from Amelia Bloomer, a feminist who attracted a lot of attention late in the nineteenth century when she advocated more freedom for women and, among other things, recommended that women wear bloomers as outergarments. However, this proposal was too daring for most women during the first quarter of the twentieth century, and the only women who took her advice were the Bloomer Girls baseball team and a few girls gym classes in some of the more advanced colleges.

The Bloomer Girls team was one of two barnstorming baseball outfits which traveled around the United States during the 1920s usually playing local All-Stars wherever they appeared. The other outfit was the House of David baseball team. Both depended on gimmicks to swell the crowd beyond what might be expected to be attracted by their display of skill at baseball. The House of David players all wore full beards, making them look like Civil War generals, while the Bloomer Girls were, of course, girls wearing bloomers. The House of

Corn Borers and Bloomer Girls

David players were generally quite competent athletes and often had one or two former big league players on their squad; these fellows had lost enough in speed and other baseball skills to drop them from even the top minor leagues, but they still were pretty good baseball players. So were the Bloomer Girls pretty good ball players—for girls, that is. The sad facts are most women simply do not have physiques well suited to the game of baseball. They may have great grace and coordination, but they just can't run as fast or throw a baseball as hard as most athletically inclined men can. Consequently, the baseball fans who came to see exhibitions by the Bloomer Girls came mostly to see those bloomers on display, and to make wise-wisecracks to and about the girl athletes.

What the Bloomer Girls lacked in baseball skills they often compensated for by superior publicity. I remember seeing one picture in the *Baltimore Sun* showing a grinning Babe Ruth swinging at and missing a third strike thrown by a Bloomer Girls pitcher in an exhibition in Birmingham, Alabama, during the baseball spring training season. By such devices the Bloomer Girls kept their name before the public, and Vic and I had both often wished we could see them play. However, they apparently never visited the Eastern Shore of Maryland during their heyday and certainly never came to Cambridge.

But since they were scheduled to be in Winsted, Connecticut, the same time we were, we decided to go see them play. Tickets were priced at fifty cents which gave us pause because we could see two or three movies for that huge amount. Nevertheless, our pent-up longings of two or three years were too much to resist, and we decided to splurge and go anyway.

It turned out to be a rather sad and drab occasion. The game was played in a small stadium down near the Mad River and a pitifully small crowd showed up—probably less than two hundred people. The promoters certainly didn't make any money, and the players probably did not receive enough to pay for their food, lodging, and travel expenses. I had seen pictures in the *Police Gazette* of the Bloomer Girls wearing red bloomers but this day they were clad in somber black garments which obviously had not been washed in recent days.

87

Before the Bridge

But the game was being played anyway and so Vic and I stationed ourselves in the stands directly behind home plate. That way we could see if the pitcher for the Bloomer Girls could throw a curve ball.

I can't remember much about the game and have no idea now whether the All-Stars or the Bloomer Girls won it, but both Vic and I were fascinated by the Bloomer Girls' catcher who had a really remarkable throwing arm and threw out three or four All-Stars trying to steal second base. The program card that day did not give last names for the Bloomer Girls who were identified only by their first names such as Mary, Ellen, Esther, Jane, etc. The only one I remember for certain was the catcher who was named Irene.

Most girls tend to lob a baseball when they throw it, but the Bloomer Girls all tossed the ball with vigor. Their throws were not "frozen ropes" of the kind Jimmy Dykes used to throw when he played third base for the Phildelphia Athletics but neither were they lobs. Even so, Irene stood out and often threw the ball back to the pitcher faster than the pitcher threw it. Her throws to second base were amazing, and Vic and I told each other that Irene had a better throwing arm than most of the catchers we had seen in organized baseball.

In fact, we marvelled at Irene for five or six innings—until one of the All-Stars fouled a ball high up in the air and right in front of us. Irene threw off her catcher's mask and pursued the ball, catching it within a few feet of where we were sitting, and then paused to wipe some dirt and perspiration from her face. Whereupon both Vic and I made a simultaneous discovery.

Irene had a beard! Not a long flowing one such as the House of David players disported, but a dense short stubble much like that of a dark bearded man who has not shaved for about two days. It was much more than any "five o'clock shadow."

Later that year I told Wilson about the bearded Bloomer Girl catcher, and he laughed. "I thought you knew," he said, "that those girls are too smart to take on a dirty job like catching. They usually have a man for both pitching and catching jobs."

We finally found some corn borers in the fields around Winsted and no doubt a red-topped pin was stuck in the map of Connecticut down at the Department of Agriculture in Washington. Our discovery gave us a mild feeling of accomplishment, but both Vic and I were happy when our second week in Winsted ended, and we headed back to Maryland to turn in our truck, even though it meant our fat salaries were ending.

The following summer Vic got a different job which permitted him to start work in June, but I returned for a second term as a hunter of corn borers. However, this second year was much less interesting than the first. For one thing I was assigned to locations entirely within Maryland during the summer of 1932 and in addition my salary was cut from twenty-eight to twenty-two dollars a week. It was still a lot of money because the depression had got even worse than it was in 1931.

Nevertheless, I was delighted when the corn borer season ended in 1932 because the last week of it had been utterly frustrating. Our team of three inspectors had been assigned first to Pocomoke City, then to Elkton, and finally to Baltimore City! This last assignment pleased one member of our team—a boy named Hurd—because he had never lived in a large city before. The new location worried our team captain greatly.

This captain, an older fellow named Ramey, was a conscientious man and it worried him because not only did we fail to find corn borers, we could not even find corn. Who made the decision to send us to Baltimore I never learned. Perhaps he was some worthy Republican administrator from New York or Chicago who thought Baltimore was a village with corn growing in its backyards, or more likely he simply confused Baltimore City with Baltimore County, where cornfields could be found. I protested that some mistake had been made but our field supervisor said his orders were clear; we were to go to Baltimore and search there for corn borers.

Before the Bridge

So we did. The first day we spent all day looking for fields of corn and found none at all. My two associates—from Ohio and West Virginia—said that as a native Marylander I should at least be able to find one cornfield in a city where the Department of Agriculture apparently believed such fields were abundant. So I asked Wilson, who was living there, for help. He told me he knew of only one and he was not sure it was within the city limits but we need not be too particular on that point. This cornfield, Wilson said, was on the grounds of the Sheppard-Pratt Hospital for the mentally ill far out on North Charles Street. So our second day we drove out there and sure enough there was a field of corn about five or ten acres in size. We got permission from the authorities to inspect it for corn borers and spent all that day and the next two going over every stalk of corn in the field. I doubt that any cornfield was ever more thoroughly inspected than that small tract on the grounds of the Sheppard-Pratt Hospital. There were no corn borers there. If there had been even one, we would have found it.

For various reasons I never returned to corn borer hunting after the summer of 1932. One reason was that the Republicans were booted out in the elections of 1932, and I suspect that any corn borer hunters in 1933 were good Democrats. However, I have watched the progress of the corn borer in the United States for half a century now and I am convinced that he is a wily insect which is in no danger of becoming extinct. He has not wiped out the American corn crop, which is today far greater than it was in 1932, but neither have all the efforts of the Department of Agriculture and the various manufacturers of insecticides wiped out the corn borer. His human enemies have tried many tricks in their attempts to exterminate him in America but the corn borer has survived them all and has shown a few tricks of his own.

One of these tricks has been to change his host crop. In recent years corn borers have been found in green beans, peppers, potatoes, and even cotton plants. Although they apparently still prefer corn to feed on, the wily corn borer will produce his frass on various other plants when corn becomes too inhospitable for any reason.

Also, it intrigues me that the Delmarva Peninsula today is reported by the Department of Agriculture to have more corn borers per acre than almost any other section of comparable size in the nation. Nevertheless, total production of corn in Delaware and on the Eastern Shore of Maryland and Virginia is many times what it was in the 1930s, and the yield per acre is more than twice what it was then. Nearly all this corn goes to feed the plump and juicy fryers and roasters which the Perdue Chicken Company sells all over the nation.

The Bloomer Girls have been extinct for nearly half a century. They were killed off by the Great Depression but if they had survived that, short shorts would have done them in.

Opera Stars and Marked Cards

ONE of the most famous of Damon Runyon's fictional Broadway characters was a gambler named Sky Masterson. Sky got his name from the fact that he was willing to risk very large sums of money on a wager. In fact, the sky was the limit; but he would bet only on his own proposition, not on those brought to him by others.

Sky's caution in accepting bets may have been learned the hard way—losses on what looked like sure things only to have the sure thing backfire. But he attributed his wisdom in such matters to some advice given to him by his father. Sky said that his father had been a poor man who was unable to endow him with working capital when he left home but instead had given him words of great wisdom. His father told him never to bet on the other person's proposition. He said that some day a stranger, holding an unopened deck of cards in his hand, would come up to Sky and offer to bet that he could cause the jack of spades to jump out of the deck and squirt cider in Sky's ear. "But, son," the father said, "do not bet him, for as sure as you do you are going to get an ear full of cider."

I never read this advice from Sky Masterson's father until about 1935, and I might not have heeded it anyway. However, if I had followed it in January of 1931, I might have been able to both see and hear Helen Jepson when she sang at Chestertown in the Washington College auditorium that year.

I had been familiar with the names of quite a few opera stars long before I came to Washington College, because my mother used them in a playful identification of the various sizes of wild blackberries which Vic, Mark, and I picked in and around the three pine forests which my father owned. The largest of all our blackberries, full-bodied, and even swollen in appearance, she called Schumann-Heink, the next largest a Galli-Curci, then a Lucrezia Bori, and finally a Mabel Garrison. Any berry smaller than a Mabel Garrison was not given any special name; they were just unnamed members of the chorus.

My mother told us that in opera it apparently took a large body to produce a truly great voice—so it didn't surprise us when we saw pictures of Madam Schumann-Heink to see that she was full-bodied indeed. That was to be expected of a great opera star and Schumann-Heink was the greatest of her day, or perhaps any other day. For this reason and because I had not liked the one recorded operatic aria which I had heard, by Galli-Curci, opera stars had very little appeal to me. I don't believe I would have been willing to pay twenty-five cents to hear any one of the four great stars listed above. Mabel Garrison might have been an exception—not for her singing ability—but only because she was the State of Maryland's first operatic star and had graduated from Western Maryland College a year or two ahead of Wilson.

Anyway, it did not excite me when the Kent County and Washington College newspapers both announced that the newest star of the N. Y. Metropolitan Opera, Helen Jepson, was going to sing at Washington College on January 20, 1931. And most of my fellow students at the college had the same lack of interest in this attempt to expose us to a splash of culture. However, all this changed dramatically when the Kent County Musical Society, which was sponsoring the event, had a picture of Miss Jepson posted on the bulletin board in William Smith Hall.

Miss Jepson had not the slightest resemblance to the broad beamed opera stars whose pictures I had seen earlier. This picture showed her in a long but low cut white gown which accentuated her many youthful feminine charms. She had light, slightly curly hair which fell almost to her bare shoulders, a full sensuous looking mouth, a perfect nose, and merry eyes. All things considered, she looked like a combination of Betty Grable, Marilyn Monroe, and Bo Derek. The male stu-

Before the Bridge

dents of Washington College, almost to a man, became lovers of music, and most of us resolved to go see and hear her sing.

I was then a sophomore living on the third floor of East Hall above the rooms occupied by Professor Dumschott and his pretty, young wife. Because Professor Dumschott's proximity had a definite inhibiting effect on the students living above him, we usually went over to Middle Hall for most of our forbidden extracurricular activities such as poker games.

Poker was strictly forbidden by the rules of the college in those days but this, of course, did not stop us from playing it. Professor Howell even said that poker was a valuable part of a college education and he often referred to it as "applied psychology and economics" which, he said, might some day become an official part of this curriculum.

On the night Miss Jepson was scheduled to sing, Charlie Holland, Reds Bullock, and I left our quarters in East Hall about an hour before the concert was scheduled to begin, and on our way over to William Smith Hall stopped in Middle Hall where we found a session in applied psychology and economics in progress. Although the weather was bitterly cold that night, the third floor poker room was hot because the power plant, in order to heat all the buildings on the campus, had to overheat those near the source of power. This was due to the fact that the underground steam lines had inadequate pressure controls. Therefore, William Smith Hall, West Hall, and Middle Hall were all overheated in order to heat East Hall and Reid Hall adequately. Anyway, the windows on the third floor of Middle Hall were open but the room was still hot, and so was the game we found in progress. The players had set a limit of five and ten cents instead of the usual penny ante.

The game looked so interesting that Charlie, Reds, and I decided to play a few hands before going on to the concert. In less than twenty minutes all three of us had been wiped out. Even the fifty-cent pieces we had set aside for student tickets to the concert were gone. Dolefully, we sat around watching the survivors continue the battle for a while, but the game was no longer fascinating to us.

Helen Jepson. The talented and beautiful opera star indirectly taught the author about marked playing cards. Courtesy Culver Pictures.

Before the Bridge

Then Charlie Holland had an inspiration. Why not go over to William Smith Hall anyway and hear Miss Jepson even if we could not see her; the hallway outside the auditorium would require no ticket. So off we went, arriving just before the intermission. We entered the front door of William Smith Hall just as Miss Jepson was about halfway through "The Rose" by Rimsky-Korsakov. But when the last note burst through the closed doors, a lady usher of the Kent County Musical Society followed swiftly behind it. In a glance she recognized us as freeloaders and fixed us with such a cold and scornful look that we quickly abandoned our pretense of reading the notices on the bulletin board and sheepishly headed toward an exit.

On our way out we stopped in a small room adjacent to the auditorium and well known to all male students. There we made a very pleasant discovery. William Smith Hall was even closer to the power plant than Middle Hall and the excess heat had caused someone to open the windows of the auditorium and the one in our small room. Through these two open windows we could hear the buzz of the audience as it waited for Miss Jepson to resume her concert. The same thought occurred to all three of us just about simultaneously. Why not stay and hear the second half? In our male sanctuary we would be perfectly safe from the scornful eyes of all lady ushers from the Kent County Musical Society.

We stayed. Miss Jepson sang three more songs and all of them came through two open windows and the few feet of still cold air between them with perfect fidelity. She closed with "The Italian Street Song" from *Naughty Marietta* and no one has ever sung it quite so well since then—not even Jeanette MacDonald inspired by Nelson Eddy and backed by a regiment of Royal Canadian Mounted Police. It was a great evening after all.

About two weeks later I asked Reds Bullock to join me in another attempt at poker on the third floor of Middle Hall.

"Maybe we can win our money back."

"Don't go. They cleaned us using marked cards when Helen Jepson was here."

Opera Stars and Marked Cards

"You are imagining things, Reds. I remember that they opened up a brand new deck just after we sat down at the table."

"I know they did, and that is what did us in. Those cards were marked by the manufacturer. I checked them out when I was over there this week. Do you remember what those cards looked like?"

"Sure, they were gray backed cards with a couple of hundred or so little wheels all over the backs. They all looked exactly alike."

"Did you count the spokes in each wheel?"

"No, the wheels were all tiny things, and the spokes were even smaller."

"Well," Reds said, "the wheels all had thirteen spokes in them. That is, all of them did except two on the back of each card. These two little wheels had only twelve spokes and the missing spoke tells what the card is. If the spoke is missing at one o'clock, it is the ace, two o'clock, it is the king, three o'clock, it is the queen, and so on all the way around the wheel. The location of the wheel itself tells whether it is a spade, heart, diamond, or club. If this wheel with a missing spoke is in the extreme left-hand corner it is a spade; if it is second from the left, it is a heart, third is a diamond, and fourth is a club. The other end of the card has a similarly located twelve-spoke wheel so you can read them from either end."

We had been playing stud poker that night Miss Jepson sang, and Reds did not have to explain to me how important it was to know exactly what card was being held face down by everyone at the table. I had believed for two weeks that I had been wiped out by too much confidence in a pair of jacks, an excess of hope in trying to fill an inside straight, or some other deficiency in experience or judgment. And it did nothing at all to increase my sense of self-confidence to learn that my failure to count the number of tiny spokes in those small wheels may have been an even bigger factor in my financial collapse that night.

I still don't know how a deck of cards could be rigged so as to cause the jack of spades to spring up and squirt cider in some unwary bettor's ear, but I have come to believe that Sky Masterson's father was right and some smart gambler has probably figured out a way to do it, even though I can't imagine how it might be done.

As for Helen Jepson, I continued to follow her career for the next ten years or so and was particularly pleased when she and John Charles Thomas scored a great success together in Pittsburgh. If she had played in Baltimore during the late 1930s, while I was living there, I certainly would have gone to see her perform but she never did. And I suspect it may be a good thing that I never got to see her in person up close. After all, it seems unlikely that any woman ever really existed who could sing like Beverly Sills and look like a combination of Bo Derek and Marilyn Monroe.

A cider-squirting jack of spades is just as easy to imagine.

ELEVEN

They All Wanted Something

O N June 11, 1932, Washington College staged a giant celebration in honor of the sesquicentennial anniversary of its founding. This celebration featured military bands, cannons, and similar trapping for such occasions, but the biggest attraction was the array of dignitaries and celebrities which came to Chestertown that day.

Among the dignitaries were two candidates for President of the United States, the German Ambassador to Washington, and Gustavus Vasa, King of Sweden. The two candidates for President, Albert C. Ritchie, Governor of Maryland, and Dr. Ray Lyman Wilbur, Secretary of the Interior under Herbert Hoover, appeared in person, along with Baron Wilhelm Friedrich Von Prittwitz und Gaffron, the German Ambassador, but Gustavus Vasa, the Swedish King, appeared only as the leading character in a pageant directed by Professor John D. Makosky of the English department. The original Gustavus Vasa had died in 1560 so that it is understandable he was not present in person.

However, it is necessary to explain why a pageant celebrating an ancient Swedish king should be staged at Chestertown, Maryland in 1932, and the explanation is a simple one. The 1932 pageant was the second time the story of Gustavus Vasa had been presented publicly by the students of Washington College. The first time was in 1784 when George Washington came to visit the new college named in his honor by the College President Dr. William Smith. Dr. Smith had thought that Gustavus, having staged a revolution which won Sweden its freedom from the tyrannical King of Denmark, was much like

Before the Bridge

George Washington who had just led his own nation to freedom from the tyrannical King of England, George III.

In describing the 1784 pageant in one of his papers Dr. Smith wrote that when the pageant was complete he had turned toward George Washington and said "behold the modern Gustavus Vasa," adding there was not "a dry eye in the audience." Could be.

If so, the 1932 pageant was not as moving as the first one had been because when it was finished, there was not a wet eye in the audience—so far as I could see. And I was in a good position to look because I was on the stage as a spear carrier in the rear ranks of the army of the villainous King of Denmark, portrayed by my classmate Mason Trupp. Mason, incidentally, was the clear star of the show, even in the role of a villain, because I have no recollection at all as to who played the part of the heroic Gustavus.

I do remember clearly that I wore one of the most ridiculous looking costumes ever to appear on any stage. It came from the Jones Costume Company in Baltimore and probably was something they had left over from a Wagnerian opera at the Lyric Theatre. I wore a musty, moldy robe of tattered burlap, but the most striking item in my outfit was a brass helmet which was too small to fit on my head, so that I was constantly afraid it would fall off and go clattering across the stage. The helmet was streaked with green copper carbonate, and my sister Carolyn, who had returned to Chestertown to see the show, said it probably had been in storage since the 1784 presentation. But as I said earlier, I was only a spear carrier with nothing to say and plenty of time to look around, and I don't believe many people were ever aware of my existence. Certainly no one ever commented to me later about my performance, one way or the other.

The speakers of the day, Governor Ritchie in the morning, Secretary Wilbur, at noon, and Baron Von Prittwitz at two o'clock, were the principal attractions that day. It was so unusual, even in those days, to have three featured speakers, that I asked Sailor Kauffman who worked in the office of President Paul E. Titsworth why Dr. Titsworth had done it.

They All Wanted Something

"It is a good question," Sailor told me, "and I asked the boss the same thing myself. He told me that he had not planned to have three speakers but had invited three in the hope that at least one of them would accept. In fact, he never invited Secretary Wilbur at all but did send an invitation to President Hoover. Hoover wrote that although he would like to attend, the press of government work would not permit him and so he was asking his longtime friend and trusted associate, Secretary Wilbur, to come in his place. Dr. Wilbur had been President of Stanford University before he became Secretary of the Interior so he would feel at home on a college campus.

"So you see," Sailor continued, "why Dr. Wilbur came. He couldn't refuse the request of his boss, the president, under any circumstances and particularly if he wanted to keep alive his hopes that Hoover would help get the Republican nomination for him in 1936. And of course Dr. Titsworth couldn't write President Hoover and tell him that if you can't come in person, we don't want anything to do with you."

Baron Von Prittwitz accepted because Dr. Titsworth had come to know him personally when he arranged to lead some groups of tourists through Germany during the 1920s before the stock market crash. Also, the baron probably thought that participation in a celebration of the founding of the first college named in honor of George Washington would be a good way to help improve relations between the United States and Germany, all of which was a part of the ambassador's job.

I already knew why Governor Ritchie had accepted Dr. Titsworth's invitation. Ritchie was an avowed candidate for president; he knew that a crowd could be expected to be present at Chestertown; and he hoped to strengthen his position as Maryland's favorite son by the exposure he would receive in the papers and newsreels which were so popular in movie houses in those days. Ritchie, of course, wanted to be the Democrat who would keep Hoover from having that second term which was so essential to Secretary Wilbur's hopes for 1936. I was fully aware of Ritchie's hopes and aspirations because I was, in fact, a member of the Ritchie for President Club which Al Baker had organized the day before the big celebration was to occur. If there had been a Hoover for President Club, I very probably would have joined it, since I came from a long line of Republicans, but with only one club available I had to settle for it.

Anyway, Governor Ritchie was a big handsome man who certainly looked like a president, and H. L. Mencken had already said he was the best qualified of all the Democratic candidates. Also, Mencken had said that Ritchie was the first real gentleman this country had produced since George Washington. But despite this extravagant praise from the Sage of Baltimore, history shows that Franklin D. Roosevelt won the Democratic nomination that year and went on to blast the hopes of Hoover in 1932 and Wilbur for 1936.

As for Ritchie, he not only lost out in 1932 but again in 1934 when he tried for a fourth term as Governor of Maryland. Mencken consoled him after the 1934 defeat by reminding him that Maryland voters, like all others, are fickle creatures who frequently elect the wrong man. In fact, Mencken said, they make a habit of doing that.

Politics aside, the real star of the speakers that day was Baron Wilhelm Von Prittwitz und Gaffron, but he was not the Baron Von Prittwitz who had been the commanding general in charge of German armies on the Eastern Front until just before the battle of Tannenberg in World War I. That Prittwitz was called "Der Dicke," or fat man, by the Germans who accused him of having lost his nerve just before he was replaced by General Von Hindenburg who went on to become a great hero in Germany when the Russians were defeated at Tannenberg.

The Von Prittwitz who came to Chestertown was the son of the fat discredited general, and he was not at all like his father in appearance. Instead of being a fat boy he was distinctly on the skinny side with hollow cheeks and sharp, even pinched, features. He seemed rather ill at ease until Dr. Titsworth, in introducing him, greeted him with a few sentences in German. At the first sound of his native tongue the ambassador's pinched face began to relax and he broke into a wide smile

The Ritchie for President Club. The man in the center in cap and gown is Al Baker, president of the club. The handsome man in striped white trousers is the candidate, Albert C. Ritchie, governor of Maryland and the first gentleman produced in America since George Washington, according to H. L. Mencken. The other handsome fellow, second from the right and with a pen in his coat pocket, is P. J. Wingate, author of this book. Others in the picture are: Mike Wallace, John Wagner, Charlie Morris, D. B. Ford, Charles M. Clark, Vince Brand, Pat Beasman, Lee Bell, Colin Hollingsworth, Charles B. Clark, Charles Holland, Alfred Gardner, Louis Goldstein, Professor Goodwin, and Marvin (Mike) Williams on the far right.

when it was announced to the assembled crowd that he was not only the Baron of Prittwitz but also of Gaffron.

The baron's English was good but I cannot remember anything he said beyond some compliments to George Washington, President Hoover, and the American people in general. Von Prittwitz received an honorary doctor of laws degree that day, the same honor which the college had awarded to Governor Ritchie and President Hoover on earlier occasions. President Hoover's honorary degree was one of a total of ninety-three which he received during his career so he probably prized it highly.

In retrospect, it seems to me that all the distinguished guests who came to Chestertown that June day wanted something but did not get it. Certainly Governor Ritchie and Secretary Wilbur never got what they wanted and Baron Von Prittwitz, if he was seeking improved German-American relations, obtained at best only a very fleeting success. This may not have been the fault of the ambassador because Adolph Hitler took full control of Germany a year later. And the Führer, from then on, behaved in such a manner that an ambassador with all the combined skills of Franklin, Disraeli, and Machiavelli could not have saved the situation for Germany.

Perhaps only the host, Dr. Titsworth, got what he wanted. That is to say, if Dr. Titsworth wanted to attract favorable attention to his one-hundred-and-fifty-year-old college and to himself then he succeeded. In his personal case it was a spectacular success.

Among the visitors to Chestertown that day were representatives of the Board of Trustees of Alfred University of New York, where Dr. Paul E. Titsworth had received his undergraduate education. These representatives were looking for a new president of Alfred University and when they returned home they promptly decided to offer the job to that distinguished alumnus who had shown them that he knew how to stage a celebration in the grand manner. It mattered little that Dr. Titsworth had received stout support from many people including Professor Fred Dumschott of the history department who had arranged to have all the bands and

They All Wanted Something

military displays present that day. The commanding general gets most of the credit when things go well and all of the blame when they go wrong. General Von Hindenburg and General Von Prittwitz illustrated both points at the battle of Tannenberg.

And so it went with Dr. Titsworth. He accepted the job at Alfred University and left Chestertown in June of 1933. Before he left he praised the area he was leaving and said the entire Eastern Shore, from Cape Charles to Elkton, was perfumed by the odor of honeysuckle in bloom.

TWELVE

The Hemingway of Chemists

CHEMISTRY appealed to me the first time I was exposed to it, but it never really grabbed me by the ear and pulled me along until I took my first course in organic chemistry during my junior year at Washington College. Precisely what made organic chemistry seem so fascinating I cannot say for certain, but it probably was a mixture of three things: the science itself and the two men who introduced me to it. The two men were Dr. Kenneth S. Buxton, newly appointed professor of chemistry at Washington College, and Dr. E. Emmet Reid, of Johns Hopkins University, who wrote the book which Dr. Buxton used as the basic text for his introductory organic chemistry course.

Buxton was probably the most enthusiastic chemist I ever met and Reid, beyond all doubt, wrote the clearest English I have ever read in the field of chemistry. I knew Buxton for a period of only five years, but Reid's trail and mine crossed, off and on, for the next forty years, ending when, at age one hundred and one, he wrote his last book called *My First One Hundred Years*.

Reid's amazing skill in English composition dawned on me slowly, but Buxton's enthusiasm for organic chemistry became evident during his first lecture on the subject and was emphasized throughout the year. He started each lecture with a piece of chalk in one hand and eraser in the other, and he always seemed a little disappointed when the bell sounded to end a session.

Dr. Buxton said that organic chemistry would explain to us why roses smelled better than skunk cabbage and why straw-

The Hemingway of Chemists

berries tasted better than spinach. He also said that organic chemistry was in its infancy since more had been learned about it in the past fifty years than in the previous fifty thousand, and that probably ten times as much would be learned in the next fifty years as had been learned in the past fifty. He said we were getting in on the ground floor, and this made it all sound very exciting.

The comparative high merit of Dr. Reid's prose was not immediately evident to me. All I knew at first was that his textbook was exceedingly easy to understand and that one topic flowed smoothly and logically into the next. Every new term was explained fully when it first appeared, and every sentence was perfectly clear in meaning.

During the course of the first term Dr. Buxton frequently repeated his claim that organic chemistry was just getting started and urged us to read the chemical journals so that we would keep up to date with new developments as they were reported. After several such urgings I dutifully got out some recent copies of the *Journal of the American Chemical Society* and made two pleasant discoveries. First, I noticed that E. E. Reid was the author of many articles in this journal, and second, that every one of his pieces was written in the same clear style which he had used in writing our textbook, *College Organic Chemistry*. I mentioned this to Dr. Buxton one day and he smiled broadly.

"I'm glad you noticed that," he said. "Dr. Reid writes clearer English than any other chemist I know. That is the reason I chose his textbook for the course. Too many chemists write like Germans. Some of them even save their verbs for the end of the sentence, which may be fine for Germans but it doesn't help an American to understand what he is reading. Nearly all chemists load up their sentences with parenthetical thoughts which often become so numerous and involved that the reader forgets what it is all about before he gets to the end of a sentence. And sometimes I have had the feeling that the author did too. Reid never does that. He writes in short clear sentences which anyone can understand. Perhaps organic chemists all over the world are suffering from the fact that the greatest masters of organic chemistry have nearly all been German, but all of them, even the French, do it to some extent."

He went on to tell me that he had two books which illustrated very well how skillful Reid was in presenting chemistry in clear and simple English. "I first read Paul Sabatier's book on catalysis in French," he said, "and I thought it was well written until I came across Reid's translation of the same book. He shortened it by a third and never omitted a single significant thought. In fact, he cleared up several pages which I never had been able to figure out in Sabatier's original book. He also omitted some pages entirely simply because Sabatier had engaged in some flights of fancy which may have delighted his Gallic readers but did nothing for me, and apparently had the same effect on Reid."

During the 1931-1932 academic year I developed a growing respect and admiration for E. E. Reid, both because of the way he wrote and the large contribution he apparently was making to that growth of organic chemistry which Dr. Buxton spoke of so often. I resolved that if I ever got a chance I would try to meet Reid personally.

Although I graduated from Washington College as a mathematics major, there was never any doubt in my mind, after 1932, that I would eventually become a chemist. I stayed a math major only because of Dean Jones. There was only one dean at Washington College in those days and Dean J. S. William Jones was an influential man who was advisor to all students. He was like Dr. Buxton in at least one respect; he thought his own subject—mathematics, in this case—was of supreme importance.

Because I had scored well in the mathematics placement test for freshmen, he advised me from the start that I should major in mathematics, and so I did. This decision seemed like a wise one when I found analytical geometry to be a subject almost as fascinating as chemistry, and when Dean Jones and I began to throw Latin phrases at each other from time to time

The Hemingway of Chemists

when we met on the campus. I liked the Dean, and he apparently liked me.

When I told him that I wanted to major in a science, Dean Jones had a ready answer. "Mathematics is a science," he said. "In fact, it is the most basic science of them all, and if you really want to be a scientist, you should major in it."

The Dean's advice to me was tinged, at least to some extent I believe, by his own interests because he talked me into dropping physics from my senior year program. Under his advice, I replaced it with astronomy and surveying, two courses which he taught and which often did not have enough demand to justify a class. The result was that I graduated with a major in mathematics, a minor in chemistry, and no credits at all in physics. This would later on plague me in graduate school and force me to do makeup work in physics, but for years I probably was the only chemist with the Du Pont Company who could identify Betelgeuse in a darkened sky at night and run a line of levels next day. I'm not sure that any of my associates knew of that distinction, and I doubt they would have envied me if they did, but there it was anyway.

When I graduated from college in 1933, the Great Depression was at its deepest point and unemployment was at a peak point. Therefore, it was a piece of incredible luck for me when my sister Evelyn was able to talk Superintendent George Fox into giving me a job as a teacher of math and science in the Anne Arundel County school system. And it was a piece of even better luck when my first teaching assignment was at Brooklyn Park Junior High School, right on the edge of Baltimore. This permitted me to live in Baltimore and enjoy this magical city.

There were, I knew, a multiple of wonders in the Baghdad on the Chesapeake and one of them was Dr. E. Emmet Reid, the wizard of chemical words. So on the second Saturday of my stay in Baltimore I boarded a Charles Street bus and rode out to Homewood to see if I could meet Dr. Reid and perhaps line up a course or two which I could take under him. I found him in his office, with the door open, standing beside his desk sorting out miscellaneous papers, apparently looking for something and not finding it. When I knocked on the door, even though it was open, he looked up and said, "Yes?"

I told him that I had just graduated from college and was hoping to take some graduate courses in organic chemistry if any were given at night or on Saturday. He replied that Hopkins gave no courses in graduate chemistry at night, but that he had scheduled a seminar course in organic chemistry for Saturdays starting in the second semester and I might sign up for that. I told him that I certainly would because I thought his *College Organic Chemistry* was the most interesting book on chemistry I had ever read.

He looked at me steadily through the thick eyeglasses which gave him an owlish appearance and made no reply for what seemed like several minutes. Finally, he thanked me in a completely emotionless manner. He then went back to searching for the missing paper on his desk.

I left his office feeling that I had somehow insulted him, and I never knew until his last book appeared forty years later why he reacted the way he did that day. Nevertheless, when the second semester rolled around, I signed up for his Saturday seminar and have always been glad that I did. He spoke with the same clear simple style he used in writing but he spoke so slowly and with such apparent weariness that his lectures were not at all inspiring. Dr. Reid delivered only the first three lectures before turning the course over to several associates, and I cannot now remember what any of the lectures were about. Nevertheless, I am glad I took the course because by doing so I became an alumnus of Johns Hopkins and have enjoyed all the rights and privileges of that title for half a century. These rights and privileges consist primarily of being eligible to receive all the requests for funds which regularly go out from the university to alumni. After my one Hopkins course I switched to the University of Maryland which did offer a series of night chemistry courses at its Baltimore branch near the University Hospital.

Apparently I was not the only one to notice a weariness in Dr. Reid during the early 1930s because the university forced

The Hemingway of Chemists

him to retire in June of 1936, a year before his scheduled retirement at age sixty-five. In fact, he was given a sort of bum's rush by the university authorities. Writing about it in his autobiography he said:

> Then on the afternoon of June 30, 1936 I had a call to come to President Bowman's office. He handed me a letter telling me that I was being given leave of absence for the following year and that I was to get my things out of the chemistry laboratory under the supervision of the newly appointed director. This was only seven hours' notice.

He went on to note that his retirement pay from the university amounted to $72.98 per month, but a supplemental sum from the Carnegie pension fund for college professors gave him an additional $55.84. The total of about $129 per month, he wryly noted, "was inadequate support of my family in the style to which they would have liked to become accustomed."

So at age sixty-four Dr. Reid set out to seek additional employment. His performance during the next thirty-five years must have astonished the Hopkins authorities who apparently thought he was all washed up.

He published about as many technical papers and books during the period from 1936 to 1966 as he had in the previous thirty years, and included among the books were six volumes entitled *Organic Chemistry of Bivalent Sulfur*. This series, which began in 1958 and ended in 1966, solidified his position as the world's greatest authority on organic sulfur chemistry. And it is unlikely that he will ever be dislodged from that rank.

In addition he continued his work as a consultant for several industrial chemical concerns which emphasized research. One of these was the Du Pont Company where he remained a highly valued advisor until he was eighty-seven, and his eyesight became so poor that he could not travel to Wilmington with reasonable safety. During the last seventeen years of his consulting work with Du Pont, I was also working with the same company, in various capacities, and saw Dr. Reid frequently. I also saw him at meetings of the American Chemical Society and learned that he had developed one of the most remarkable "research circuits" in the history of chemistry.

After Hopkins pushed him out Dr. Reid became research advisor for ten colleges and universities in the South and visited each four times a year. Included among them were the universities of Richmond, Emory, South Carolina, Furman, Birmingham Southern, Howard, Alabama, Chattanooga, and J. B. Stetson, along with Marshall College and Georgia Tech. At all of these schools he gave advice to both students and faculty on how to organize and start research programs in organic chemistry and how to proceed on specific subjects after the programs got started. More than half of them are now major research centers of organic chemistry.

Dr. Reid continued both his industrial and academic consulting work until he was in his late eighties and his writing for technical publications continued much longer. In total he wrote over two hundred books and technical articles, beginning in 1899 and ending in 1972. He obtained a U. S. Patent in 1965 when he was ninety-three years old. However, after he quit his consulting work with Du Pont, I lost track of him until a review of his last book, *My First One Hundred Years*, appeared in one of the technical journals.

Samuel Johnson once told Boswell: "A woman preaching is like a dog's walking on his hind legs. It is not done well; but you are surprised to find it done at all." When I ordered a copy of Dr. Reid's new book, written at age one hundred and one, I could not avoid thinking of Johnson's sexist remark and wondering if the Hemingway of chemistry had ended his writing career on a weak note.

It was a needless worry on my part. *My First One Hundred Years* was superbly written—fully equal in clarity and simplicity to his earlier writings. In addition, it was fascinatingly interesting. Dr. Reid's descriptions of his Baptist missionary parents and the life of a country preacher in Virginia, Kentucky, Arkansas, and South Carolina were as crisp and vivid as his chemical reporting. He knew the territory and liked it. In telling about one of his first teaching

The Hemingway of Chemists

assignments, at Baylor University in Waco, Texas, he wrote: "I arrived in Waco at Noon on a Saturday and joined the First Baptist Church at the eleven o'clock service the next day."

In another chapter he refers to an essay on cats which he composed when he was eight years old. "The original," he wrote, "in my own handwriting was kept for many years. Reading it now, I see the style is strikingly like that I have used ever since. For many years I have been trying to get away from short sentences."

Students of chemistry who will be reading his monumental work, *Organic Chemistry of Bivalent Sulfur,* for at least a few more centuries, should rejoice that he never succeeded in his efforts to get away from short sentences. Incidentally, the six volumes of this text all identify the author as Professor of Chemistry Emeritus, Johns Hopkins University. So whatever resentment Dr. Reid felt when he was forcibly retired by Hopkins in 1936 had apparently evaporated during the twenty-two years which elapsed before the first volume of this series was published.

Dr. Reid also devoted a page in his last book to his translation of Paul Sabatier's book on catalysis, *La Catalyse en Chemie Organique,* which had caught Dr. Buxton's fancy in 1932. Reid wrote:

Translating this book was one of the few smart things that I have done. It got me started as an author. I had the belief, which I hold most strongly now, that the translator should get the facts out of the words of one language and put them into the words of another. If you transfer apples from a crate into a basket, you should not bring any of the packing with them. The words are only the crate in which ideas come packed. A thorough knowledge of the subject is far more important than familiarity with the language.

Following this concept, he wrote at an earlier date another book called *Chemistry Through The Language Barrier* which gives chemists many useful hints about how to scan chemical articles in all major languages except Chinese.

Before the Bridge

His last book was interesting throughout its two hundred pages, but for me the most interesting thing of all was a short paragraph on his textbook which I had first seen in my junior year at Washington College. This paragraph fascinated me because it explained, I believe, why he stared at me so coldly when I complimented him on the book which had introduced me to organic chemistry. Concerning this book, *College Organic Chemistry*, he wrote:

> This is the book which I should not have written. It cost me a lot of time but added nothing to my fame or fortune. The royalties I received from it balanced almost exactly the money I spent on it for assistance. My time could have been put to better advantage.

You never can tell about such things.

THIRTEEN

Baghdad on the Chesapeake

THE Baltimore of 1933 was a marvelous place. Beyond doubt it had thousands of people who were without work or money and were consequently living lives of quiet desperation. I knew some of them personally. But for a twenty-year-old boy with a job, fresh from college and the Eastern Shore of Maryland, it was a place of magic with more delights and wonders than ever had existed in Athens, Rome, or even Camelot.

Baltimore seemed to me to be a modern Baghdad crammed full of all sorts of things which interested me, including good things to eat, pretty girls, theatres, both legitimate and otherwise, libraries, seats of learning, steel mills, chemical plants, athletic contests of all sorts, and a waterfront fairly dripping with the extracts and distillates from the markets of the rest of the world.

This Baltimore waterfront alone was an amazing sight which began, for incoming visitors traveling by water, with Sparrows Point on the right and Curtis Bay on the left and ended with Fort McHenry on the left and the McCormick Spice Company dead ahead, just beyond the wooden piers and wharves where the Bay ferries and steamboats docked. At night the steel mills at Sparrows Point regularly put on a fireworks display with so much light and color that it took a good imagination to have the display equalled by "the rockets' red glare, the bombs bursting in air" above Fort McHenry. The freighters and tankers anchored in Curtis Bay were not as glamorous as the real lights of Sparrows Point or the imaginary ones at Fort McHenry, but they all did their bit in making Baltimore seem like a Baghdad on the Chesapeake to me. So did the aromas which came from the McCormick Spice Company making the area around the intersection of Pratt and Light streets smell like a Christmas bakeshop with nutmeg, cloves, and ginger all intermingled.

Baltimore foods, incidentally, gave me two of my biggest surprises during my first year in Baghdad on the Chesapeake. I had been led to believe that Eastern Shore cooks knew more about how to prepare seafood for the table than city chefs no matter how sophisticated the latter might be. Consequently, it surprised me when I ate the best fried oysters I had ever tasted in the Eastern Shore Room of the Southern Hotel and the best crab imperial ever produced anywhere, in Miller Brothers Restaurant on Fayette Street in Baltimore. In fifty years of searching I have never found its equal. The Rennert Hotel, which was famous as a sort of headquarters for Eastern Shoremen visiting Baltimore, had a reputation for serving good seafood, but it was on its last legs in 1933 and was torn down a few years later. In any event, nothing came close to the Southern Hotel's fried oysters or Miller Brothers' crab imperial.

The Southern's fried oysters were obviously cooked in deep fat because they came out with a uniform tan color and a taste which proved the purchasing agent knew where to obtain oysters which were fat and salty. The ones the Southern served may have come from Chincoteague Bay, but more likely they came from the lower part of the Chesapeake—somewhere in the region extending from Holland Island to Norfolk. No treatment known to man could make an oyster taken from that part of the Chesapeake lying north of the Choptank River taste like those fried oysters served in the Eastern Shore Room of the Southern Hotel during my first year in Baltimore.

The secret of Miller Brothers' crab imperial has remained a mystery to me. A blue crab tastes like a blue crab whether caught in the brackish waters at the mouth of the Chester River or in the salty ocean waters where the Chesapeake flows into the Atlantic. The only absolute requirement for good taste is that the crab be fat at the time of capture. Miller Brothers obviously used crab meat from fat crabs, but they did

Baghdad on the Chesapeake

something beyond that in producing their matchless product. Their crab imperial was about ninety-eight percent lump crab meat with just enough binder of some sort to hold the lumps together—without the bits of pepper, potato, celery, onion, and other things which people who don't understand what they are doing sometimes put in crab imperial. The finished product served by Miller Brothers was a rounded heap of lump crab meat baked so that the outer lumps were a golden brown, about one shade lighter than the Southern's fried oysters. If I had been making twice my monthly salary of $120, I would have eaten fried oysters and crab imperial more often. As it was, I ate most of my breakfasts and dinners at the rooming house where I lived—1010 Cathedral Street. Mrs. Morris, who ran this fascinating place, was a fine cook, but she specialized in chicken and beef rather than seafood. When I ate out, I usually went to one of the Oriole cafeterias, particularly the one on North Avenue. This particular Oriole had a man and woman team which specialized in serving coffee.

The male member of this team, a fellow of about thirty I guess, poured coffee, and his female companion added the cream. Their performance was so remarkable that people visited this Oriole just to have coffee. The coffee was served at the diner's table after the other food had been selected and a table located. The coffee pourer started his pot flowing three or four inches above the cup and then swept his arm upward in a smooth easy motion which produced a stream of coffee about two feet long, filling the coffee cup about eighty percent when it all got settled away. Then the cream pourer did the same thing with a smaller pot and a thinner stream of cream, leaving almost no freeboard when the show was all over. How many patrons got scalded with hot coffee while the coffee pourer was perfecting his act I never heard. All the demonstrations I watched went off exactly as planned.

While Baltimore was filled with wonders, the football season provided me with my most exciting moments during the first three months of my first year in Baghdad on the Chesapeake. Maryland had three excellent football teams in 1933—

Before the Bridge

Western Maryland College, the University of Maryland, and the U. S. Naval Academy—but only the Navy team was ranked among the national football powers. Western Maryland and Maryland were coached by Dick Harlow and Curley Byrd, respectively, and both of these men were inventive masters of the game who knocked off nationally ranked football teams from time to time. In a few years Harlow would be lured away by Harvard, and Byrd would become President of the University of Maryland, but their rivalry was at its peak during the early 1930s. Nevertheless, even when Maryland played Western Maryland in Baltimore Stadium, the game would draw only ten or fifteen thousand fans, while Navy would attract crowds of fifty to sixty thousand when the midshipmen played such teams as Notre Dame, Ohio State, and Yale.

Using free tickets provided by Wilson, I watched Navy, Maryland, or Western Maryland each Saturday during the football season of 1933 except for one—October 21—when I went to Chestertown to see Franklin D. Roosevelt receive an honorary degree from Washington College. It was this same Roosevelt who had just changed the rules governing the football competition between Army and Navy—the two teams which provided the climax of my 1933 football season.

Army and Navy no longer have the kinds of football teams which both fielded during the 1920s and 1930s, and so their annual game is no longer as glamorous as it was in those days. During the two decades from 1920 to 1940 the Army-Navy game frequently produced some of the most exciting football seen in the country and their annual battle was nearly always the most colorful athletic contest of the year. The 1924 and 1926 Army-Navy games, held in Baltimore and Chicago, respectively, excited football fans all over the nation and had special interest for me. My mother, Aunt Kate, and my two sisters, Evelyn and Carolyn, had all gone to see the 1924 game in Baltimore's new Memorial Stadium, and had seen Cadet Edgar Garbisch win the game for Army by kicking four field goals and thus doing all the scoring in Army's 12 to 0 victory. Then in the 1926 Chicago game Army managed to tie Navy 21 to 21, even though Navy won all its other games and also won the national championship that year.

Navy attributed part of its persistent trouble in beating Army, during the 1920s, to Army's practice of recruiting All-American football players from colleges and universities with strong teams, and then giving these established stars three more years of varsity competition at West Point. The Navy authorities cited such Army heroes as Harry Wilson and Chris Cagle, who had been authentic All-Americans at other institutions before entering West Point, but there were many others even though they were less celebrated. All this irked the Navy so much that after losing to Army in 1927, following the 1926 tie suffered by their national championship team, the midshipmen broke off the series and refused to play Army until it adopted eligibility rules similar to Navy's.

So there were no Army-Navy football games in 1928 and 1929, to the great disappointment of football fans all over the nation. The series was resumed in 1930 at President Hoover's request because he thought the color, glamour, and excitement might help lift the nation out of its doldrums. However, the Army held onto its old eligibility rules and kept right on beating the Navy. Then when President Roosevelt took office in 1933 he decided, probably partly at least because he considered himself to be a "Navy man," that in the future both service academies should have the same eligibility rules for football players—the Navy's rules.

This then was the background for my first Army-Navy football game—a game which pulled together on one day all the glamour which I had perceived in football ever since I had started to read about it in the exciting columns which Grantland Rice and Wilson wrote on this most exciting of all college games. My delight at the prospect of seeing the most glamorous game of the 1933 football season was heightened by the fact that Wilson had arranged to have his paper, the *Baltimore News*, pay me to record statistics on the game—number of first downs, average length of punts, number of passes, etc. This meant that I not only had a free ticket but also had my transportation to Philadelphia paid for, a seat in the press box, and was paid five dollars for my day's work. It was like paying a ten-year-old boy five dollars to work in a candy store which had already given him unlimited sampling privileges.

When I met Wilson at about nine-thirty in the morning in the Pennsylvania Station on Charles Street, he had copies of four newspapers under his arm: the *Baltimore News, Baltimore Sun, Washington Star,* and *New York Herald-Tribune.* As soon as we boarded the train, he handed me his copy of the *News* and said: "Here, you can read what I have already written about the game while I catch up on the competition."

I was surprised to notice that Wilson's story in the *News* began on the front page and was written as if we were already in Philadelphia and at the scene of the game. He said that early arrivals were beginning to show up at Franklin Field and were being greeted by a swarm of vendors offering to sell them pennants, programs, papers, hot dogs, and various other things. Because I knew Wilson had not been in Philadelphia earlier that morning, I asked him if it wasn't risky to be describing something he had not yet seen.

"Not really," he said. "This is the morning edition of the paper which you are reading. I picked it up down at the office, but it won't hit the streets here until about eleven, and by that time we will be in Philadelphia. If somebody has blown up the stadium, I'll just call the paper and have them hold back this edition. But the chances are, a million to one, that the real scene will be just the way I wrote it up last night. It looked that way last year, and it will be the same thing next year. By noon the people in Baltimore will be wondering what it looks like in Philadelphia, and this story tells them. You'll notice that I pretty much stuck to generalities. I talk about the gold braid arriving later, and I don't mention any names among the early arrivals. This way, I won't be wrong if one of the high ranking admirals or generals breaks a leg and never does make it to the game."

When we arrived in Philadelphia and took a cab out to Franklin Field it was about eleven thirty, and the scene looked almost exactly as Wilson had described it. The place was swarming with vendors, but there were only a few hundred people in the stadium. However, the crowd soon began to arrive, and by the time midshipmen and cadets marched in, just about every seat in the place was filled except for the two sections set aside for the marchers. Even the seats behind the steel uprights were filled, and the press box was jammed with reporters and their assistants.

Wilson had his personal telegrapher seated on his right while I, as statistician, was seated on his left. In addition to the reporters and their assistants, there were present in the press box about a dozen midshipmen and an equal number of army cadets. These young fellows were there to identify members of their respective teams and give other information to the reporters as the game progressed.

The game started at 1:00 P.M. and Wilson had his first deadline at 1:30. He had to wire a lead paragraph on the current status of the game for the 2:00 P.M. edition of the *News* which would be on the streets at about 2:30. He had another deadline at 3:30 for the final Saturday edition of the *News*, but he also had to give a current status report for the first edition of the Sunday *American* which usually hit the streets at 6:30 P.M.

The game itself was all I had expected it might be. Army scored the first touchdown but missed the point and so led 6 to 0. Navy came right back with a touchdown of its own and made good the point thereby going ahead by a 7 to 6 score. The cadets in the press box had shown considerable excitement when Army made its score but their display of jubilation was nothing compared to what the midshipmen did when they went ahead by that one point. All twelve of them, who had been spread out the length of the press box, came together near the middle and began the wildest display of excitement I have ever seen at a football game. They pounded each other on the back, leaped into the air singly, in pairs, in small groups, and finally all at the same time, all the while screaming at the top of their voices. This went on for five or six minutes until the reporters who had been trying to ask them for information finally gave up and turned to the programs for answers to their questions.

Before the Bridge

Unhappily for the midshipmen their lead was only temporary, and Army won again as it had done in every game played since 1926. Navy had to wait until 1934 for its first triumph against Army in over a decade. I saw the 1934 game too and Navy was jubilant that year also but not as wildly so as they had been with that 7 to 6 lead in 1933. Nor, I suspect, have any of Navy's many victories, which in recent years finally gave them the lead in their long rivalry with Army, produced quite so much wild excitement as that temporary lead did in 1933. However, I doubt that any midshipman would willingly go back to the days, prior to Franklin D. Roosevelt, when victory over Army in football was so sweet because it was so rare.

After Wilson completed all his running reports for the various editions of the *News* and *Sunday American,* he wrote a "color story" about the game for the Hearst International Press, and it was eight that night before we left Franklin Field. Wilson, his telegrapher, and I were the last three people to leave the stadium; even the trash collectors had gone earlier. We arrived in Baltimore about eleven and ate dinner at Hasslingers Restaurant near the railroad station. The long day did not cause me to lose my enthusiasm for football, but Wilson's job never again seemed to me to be just a paid holiday.

During the months of December and January I had free tickets to a wide assortment of athletic events including soccer, basketball, boxing, wrestling, and ice hockey, but none of these sports was as exciting and glamorous as football. However, I was impressed by the quality of the soccer games played in East Baltimore. They played a ball control game which was far different from the soccer I had seen on the Eastern Shore, where the general idea of every player seemed to be that he should kick the ball as far as he could every time he got near it.

I also went to see quite a few movie and vaudeville shows at the Century and Hippodrome theaters, but not as many as I would have liked to see because I had to pay for the tickets to these glamorous places. Nevertheless, when Bill Robinson played at the Hippodrome I went to see him because I had just missed him in Trenton, New Jersey, when I was searching for corn borers in Morrisville, Pennsylvania, just across the Dela-

Baghdad on the Chesapeake

ware River, in 1931. I also went to see Eleanor Powell when this long-legged dancing beauty appeared at the Century Theatre. So within a period of about two months I saw, in person, probably the only two dancers in history who could go tap for tap with Fred Astaire. Baghdad on the Chesapeake was indeed a marvelous place during the first six months of my stay there.

However, Baltimore was not all glamour for me even so. During this same period I was working at the job which permitted me to live in Baltimore—teaching mathematics and general science at the Brooklyn Park Junior High School.

My teaching job was uneventful, and I had no real trouble with the problem which plagues most young teachers— keeping order in the classroom. There were a number of reasons why this was so. The students at Brooklyn Park came mostly from hard working families who believed that education would make life easier for their children, and so parents urged their offspring to take their school work seriously. And most of them did, because this was well ahead of the time when it became popular for students to walk up the down staircase as a means of asserting their independence. An even more important factor was the principal of the Brooklyn Park school systems—Mrs. James Bourke. Mrs. Bourke, a master psychologist, had established herself with both the young and old in the Brooklyn area, and none dared to take a stand against her. She believed that order in the classroom was absolutely necessary for learning to take place, and she had established order long before I appeared on the scene. She could look a kid in the eye and tell in a fifth of a second if he was lying, and when he was, she then could fix him with a look that was so potently sudorific that he was dripping with perspiration in five or ten seconds. Finally, I was coach of the soccer team, and that position automatically carried with it a certain amount of respect or even awe.

Anyway, I had an uneventful year in the classroom and both the high and low point of it occurred on the same day in January. It was a high point for the students and my own low point.

I was demonstrating to a general science class how to

generate acetylene from calcium carbide and water, and everything went well at first. The procedure is a simple one. Water is dripped through a funnel onto powdered calcium carbide in a flask. The resulting acetylene is carried from the flask by means of a glass tube through the same rubber stopper which holds the funnel used to introduce the water. The presence of the acetylene is shown by putting a lighted match to the end of the exit tube and watching the acetylene burn with a sooty flame.

As I said, all went well at first until the funnel ran out of water and the acetylene stopped escaping, causing the flame to go out. The students watched all this with mild interest, but when I added more water and relighted the escaping acetylene gas, the whole apparatus blew up with a bang which splattered the funnel with its tube and rubber stopper against the ceiling. Whereupon the entire class gave the experiment their total attention and several of them exclaimed: "Do that again, Mr. Wingate."

I was too dazed to explain to them that I had not intended to do it the first time. Fortunately, no one was even slightly injured, but I had nightmares for several weeks about the possibility that I might have blinded myself along with several of the students. Veterans in the handling of acetylene could surely point out several mistakes in my procedure, but they should remember that acetylene is a very tricky chemical which has blown up on far more experienced chemists than I was then. The Du Pont Company, which used hundreds of millions of pounds of acetylene in the manufacture of neoprene finally went to a new process for neoprene when it found that even the most elaborate safety procedures could not keep acetylene and its derivatives from blowing up from time to time. I was in charge of Du Pont's neoprene manufacture at the time the decision was made to abandon acetylene and go to a new process, and I heartily approved the decision although I never mentioned that 1934 blowup at Brooklyn Park.

Baghdad on the Chesapeake

Even with free tickets to all sorts of athletic events and the arrival of the beautiful Eleanor Powell on the stage of the Century, January and February were a letdown from the excitement of the football season. But all that changed when spring arrived, and the lacrosse season began.

At the invitation of Coach Keech, I joined the Mt. Washington Lacrosse Club and had the extended pleasure of playing all spring for the top lacrosse team in the nation. We played the best college teams in the country and beat them all. It was a far cry from my Washington College lacrosse days when we were lucky to beat Lehigh and Lafayette while losing to Swarthmore and New York University.

Let me say at once that Mt. Washington's supremacy that year was in no way due to my presence on the squad. The Wolf Pack, as Mt. Washington has been called for over fifty years, was loaded with former All-Americans from most of the good college teams in the country. There were nine or ten graduates of Johns Hopkins who had played on the Hopkins Olympic team of 1932 and included among them were such future Hall of Fame stars as Fritz Stude, Lorne Guild, and Jack Turnbull, perhaps the best lacrosse player of all time. There was also Jack's brother, Doug Turnbull, who had been four times chosen All-American during his college years at Johns Hopkins. Finally, there were Fred Stieber and Willie Pugh, two of the best lacrosse players ever turned out by the University of Maryland. Mt. Washington was two-deep in great lacrosse players for every position on the team. It was not surprising that we won all our games.

My personal highlight of the lacrosse season came when we played Yale. There had never been any doubt that Mt. Washington would defeat Yale and after the regulars had built up a comfortable lead, our coach sent me in at midfield to replace Doug Turnbull. Whereupon the young Yalie assigned to play opposite me came up and asked if I would give him some pointers on how midfield should be played. Such was the reputation of Mt. Washington in those days! No doubt his coach had told him that Yale should use the Mt. Washington game to learn some things which would help them later on. And perhaps it did, because Yale finished second in the Ivy League that year.

It would be easy for me to pick out the least pleasant of the four seasons of my first year in Baltimore. That was the summer of 1934 when I almost dissolved in perspiration while working in the Epsom salts factory. But it would be difficult to pick out the most pleasant. The fall of 1933, with the football season climaxed by my first Army-Navy game, was glamorous and exciting, and the spring of 1934, playing with an undefeated lacrosse team, was pleasant all the way, but winter may have been the best of them all. Not only did the talented and beautiful Eleanor Powell come to the Century Theatre, but in January I made a discovery which has given me great pleasure every year since then.

I went down three blocks from my rooming house at 1010 Cathedral Street to the Enoch Pratt Free Library and there discovered the Sage of Baltimore, H. L. Mencken.

FOURTEEN

The Sage of Baltimore

BY 1925 H. L. Mencken had been famous all over the United States for a number of years. This fame was due primarily to his books and the magazines he had edited but also partly because of his newspaper work. He wrote regularly for the *Baltimore Evening Sun* and occasionally for the *Morning Sun,* or simply the *Sun* as it was usually called.

The *Sun* was the only paper which my father subscribed to, and I read it regularly—but only the sports pages. Consequently, I had never heard of Mencken until the famous 1925 Scopes Monkey Trial began to receive a lot of attention in the *Sun* and thus became a topic for discussion by my parents.

The monkey trial got its name from the fact that John T. Scopes, a teacher in the public schools of Tennessee, had been indicted for violating the state law against teaching the theory of evolution in Tennessee public schools. Newspapers all over the country simplified the issue by declaring that the theory of evolution claimed that man had ascended, or descended, from monkeys. Clarence Darrow came in to help defend Scopes and William Jennings Bryan came to assist the prosecution in its efforts to convict him. Mencken and a host of other reporters descended on Dayton, Tennessee, to report the course of events. The reporters, Mencken in particular, had a field day. Since Scopes was convicted and fined one hundred dollars, the whole thing is now generally regarded as much ado about nothing, when it is remembered at all, but in 1925 it was front page news for several weeks.

My mother disapproved of the Scopes trial and I had a vague impression that she also disapproved of Mencken who was writing most of what the *Sun* reported on the trial. She said

Before the Bridge

Lizette Woodworth Reese was right when she called Mencken a "bad boy," although I suspect my mother may have generated the same idea all on her own. She was an admirer of Dr. Howard A. Kelly, one of the Big Four of medicine at Johns Hopkins Hospital, because he was a professional and practicing Christian and she resented Mencken's scoffing at religion. Mencken also scoffed at Dr. Kelly for his religious views but liked and admired him for his skill as a surgeon. Kelly had a similar reaction to Mencken and the two of them carried on a friendly feud for many years.

While my mother deplored the monkey trial in every way, my father was rather amused by it and said that Mencken was just about right in most of what he wrote concerning it. My father's reaction intrigued me because I knew that his favorite newspaper man was Frank R. Kent who regularly wrote a front page column called "The Great Game of Politics," and he seldom spoke well of any other newspaper reporter. So after he made several amused and favorable comments about Mencken I asked him how Mencken compared with his favorite, Mr. Kent. "Kent is a far better man," he said. "Even though there is often a lot of truth in what Mencken writes. At heart he is a joker."

Perhaps partly because of these mildly discouraging attitudes on the part of my parents I never read any of Mencken's pieces in the *Sun* until the 1928 presidential campaign. I did read some of the things he wrote about Al Smith and rather liked them. I also read a few more things by Mencken during my four years at Washington College and became a mild Mencken fan. His gleeful bombast and wild exaggeration appealed to me, partly because it never seemed to me that he expected his readers to take the exaggeration literally and because there was no malice evident in even his fiercest assaults. For example, when he declared that all ex-presidents of the United States should be hanged "as a matter of public decorum and sanitation," I never believed he was serious about this proposal! Likewise, when I came across something he had written about President Harding, claiming that Harding wrote the worst English he had ever encountered, "setting

The Sage of Baltimore

aside a college professor or two and half a dozen dipsomania-cal newspaper reporters," I once again thought he was joking as my father had suggested. After all, I had myself seen worse English than anything Harding ever wrote.

Nevertheless, despite my growing liking for Mencken, when I moved to Baltimore in 1933, I had never read any of his books and looked upon him as a sort of local phenomenon of no great significance.

All that changed swiftly following a visit I made to the Enoch Pratt Free Library one snowy evening late in 1933 after the football season ended. I asked a young lady at the desk if she had any books by H. L. Mencken. She gave me a quick, faintly amused look and said: "Yes. What are you interested in?"

"Anything. Give me his best known book."

This time she looked me over more carefully and said: "Well, that would be *The American Language* but maybe we should start you on something else." Whereupon she left and in a few minutes came back with two small books with a bookmark in each.

"Start with the ones I have marked," she said, and within half an hour my admiration for both Mencken and her judgment had become immense. She had marked "The Feminine Mind" and "The Art Eternal," two of the Sage of Baltimore's most timeless and marvelously constructed essays.

"The Feminine Mind" was the first chapter in a book called *In Defense of Women* which consisted, for the most part, of an attack on men, showing that, by comparison at least, women were very superior human beings. It started with:

A man's women folk, whatever their outward show of respect for his merit and authority, always regard him secretly as an ass, and with something akin to pity. His most gaudy sayings and doings seldom deceive them; they see the actual man within and know him for a shallow and pathetic fellow.

Before the Bridge

After developing this general theme for a few more paragraphs Mencken reached a high point. He went on:

> That it should be necessary at this late stage in the senility of the human race, to argue that women have a fine and fluent intelligence, is surely an eloquent proof of the defective observation, incurable prejudice, and general imbecility of their lords and masters.

I learned later that this device of praising one person or group by attacking its opposite was one of Mencken's old tricks, but it was new to me and I found it to be delightful, partly because I thought he was joking to an extent but also partly because there was a solid core of truth to what he was saying. He then proceeded to show that both business and professional men were sadly lacking in intellectual capacity and performance.

> No observant person indeed can come into close contact with the general run of business and professional men—I confine myself to those who seem to get on in the world and exclude the admitted failures—without marveling at their intellectual lethargy, their incurable ingenuousness, their appalling lack of ordinary sense.

On the other hand, he noted, women rebel at practicing the petty bag of tricks which men use to bring success in their endeavors and cite as proof of their intelligence.

> A chimpanzee could be trained to do the same sort of thing, but women excel in occupations which require real intelligence such as being a nurse for the sick, since this kind of work requires ingenuity, quick comprehension, courage in the face of novel and disconcerting situations and, above all, a capacity for penetrating any dominant character; and whenever she comes into competition with men in the arts, particularly on those secondary planes where nimbleness of mind is unaided by the master strokes of genius, she holds her own invariably.

The Sage of Baltimore

He closed this first chapter as forcefully as he began it, after demonstrating that women's intuition, which most men recognized as a fact of nature, was nothing but a clear indication of a superior basic intelligence.

> Intuition? Bosh! Women, in fact, are the supreme realists of the race. Apparently illogical, they are the possessors of a rare and subtle superlogic. Apparently whimsical, they hang onto the truth with a tenacity which carries them through every phase of its incessant, jelly-like shifting of form. . . . Men, too, sometimes have brains. But it is a rare, rare man, I venture, who is as steadily intelligent, as constantly sound in judgment, as little put off by appearances, as the average woman of forty-eight.

A good case can be made for the argument that Mencken was one of the early feminists because, idiotic as it may sound today, there was a time, not too long ago, when men did regard themselves as lords and masters of women and also believed that the feminine sex lacked the capacity for original and important mental activity. As a result women were excluded from nearly all graduate schools, particularly in America, and even most of the elite undergraduate schools.

Mencken surely was aware that Johns Hopkins University in his native Baltimore had refused to admit Dr. M. Carey Thomas and Dr. Christine Ladd-Franklin into its graduate school simply because they were females. Both of these remarkable women were forced to go to Europe to obtain their Ph.D. degrees before going on to distinguished careers in education and science.

Dr. Thomas was academic dean and later president of Bryn Mawr College. She was dean at Bryn Mawr when Woodrow Wilson was a professor of history there and crossed swords with the future president of the United States on several occasions. They simply did not like each other. All of which must have increased Mencken's opinion of Dr. Thomas's intelligence because his reaction to Wilson was exactly the same as hers.

Before the Bridge

Dr. Christine Ladd-Franklin, after being rejected by Hopkins, went to Germany to obtain her Ph.D. and became a philosopher of world renown, universally accepted as one of the greatest color theorists of all time, ranking with Helmholtz, Maxwell, and Newton. The world's ranking color theorist of today, Dr. Edwin Land, founder of the Polaroid Corporation, says that even today, nearly a century after Dr. Ladd-Franklin did her work, her theory of color holds up well. Forty years after Hopkins refused to grant Christine Ladd-Franklin a degree, even though she had done all the work required for a Ph.D. in mathematics, the University did invite her back, in 1926, to receive an honorary degree. This was done before I had any real knowledge of Mencken and if he made any comment on this change of heart by Hopkins, I have never been able to find it. However, I am convinced he must have agreed with Baltimore's newspaper woman, Anne Kinsolving, when she wrote:

Is Johns Hopkins University now conferring an honor upon Mrs. Christine Ladd-Franklin or is Mrs. Christine Ladd-Franklin conferring an honor upon Johns Hopkins University?

When Mencken collected what he considered to be his best writings into a book called *A Mencken Chrestomathy,* he included "The Feminine Mind" in it, but he changed the last line from "the average woman of forty-eight" to "the average multipara of forty-eight." The use of the word "multipara" in place of "woman" probably puzzled some of his readers just as the word "chrestomathy" did, but as Mencken wrote in the introduction to his *Chrestomathy,* he was not concerned with:

such ignoramuses, and I do not solicit their patronage. Let them continue to recreate themselves with whodunits and leave my vocabulary to me and my customers, who have all been to school.

The Sage of Baltimore

Mencken apparently thought that a woman who had studied several children closely for a number of years probably had accumulated some wisdom unknown to a childless member of her sex, and therefore replaced "woman" with "multipara" in the interest of greater preciseness.

The second essay which the girl at the Pratt desk had marked for me, "The Art Eternal," from *Prejudices,* Fourth Series, was a philosophical discussion of lying, and the title indicated Mencken's belief that it was a universal art. In fact, he quoted the Psalmist as the authority for this belief which he really thought needed no proof. Lying was, he said, not only universal but an absolute need of the human race.

> The great majority of us—all in brief who are normal—pass through life in constant revolt against our limitations, objective and subjective. Our conscious thought is largely devoted to plans and specifications for cutting a better figure in human society, and in our unconscious the business goes on more steadily and powerfully. No healthy man, in his secret heart, is content with his destiny.

Mencken then picked up the theme which he had emphasized in "The Feminine Mind" and wrote:

> No man could bring himself to reveal his true character, and above all his true limitations as a citizen and a Christian, his true meannesses, his true imbecilities, to his friends or even his wife. Honest autobiography is therefore a contradiction in terms: the moment a man considers himself he tries to gild and fresco himself.

That is to say, he lies. And he continued:

> The man who is most respected by his wife is the one who makes this projection most vivid—that is, the one who is the most daring and ingratiating liar.

Some people are pushed harder toward lying than others, Mencken said, but "pushed we all are." Consequently, he concluded, liars should be treated with considerable tolerance. He noted that there properly are laws against lying under oath in courts but called attention to the fact that even this practice has some merit at times. He cited King Edward VII of England as a case in point. This court case involved Edward VII when he was still Prince of Wales. Mencken wrote:

> Summoned into a court of law, to give expert testimony regarding some act of adultery, he lied like a gentleman, as the phrase goes, to protect a woman. The lie to be sure was intrinsically worthless; no one believed that the lady was innocent. Nevertheless, every decent Christian applauded the perjurer for his good intentions, including even the judge on the bench, sworn to combat false witness by every resource of forensics.

Mencken explained that not only was lying inevitable and universal but the world had little liking for habitual truth tellers. This was particularly true in the United States, he said, and went on to write my all-time favorite of Mencken quotations.

> The men the American people admire most extravagantly are the most daring liars; the men they detest most violently are those who tell the truth. A Galileo could no more be elected President of the United States than he could be elected Pope of Rome. Both high posts are reserved for men favored by God with an extraordinary genius for swathing the bitter facts of life in bandages of soft illusion.

When I finished reading these two essays, I was almost bouncing in my chair and immediately signed out the two books and took them back to 1010 Cathedral Street where I finished them that night. Next day I could hardly wait to get back to the Pratt Library to get more like them. There were five more volumes entitled *Prejudices,* and all were delightful reading. Even the title appealed to me because it indicated a basic honesty on Mencken's part, suggesting that he did not want anything he said to be taken as Holy Writ.

Eventually, I even got around to the book which my feminine adviser at the Pratt desk had decided not to start me on, *The American Language.* It was different from all the other Mencken books in that it was mostly a sober discussion of how the American language had slowly diverged from its mother English until now it was a language of its own. He did not claim it was a better language—just a different one which Americans had no reason to be ashamed of. *The American Language* was typical Mencken material in one respect—every sentence was perfectly clear in meaning and it was extraordinarily easy to read for such a scholarly book. The wild exaggerations of his other books were missing, but he apparently was unable to avoid slipping in some humor and a few denunciations of groups and individuals who irked him.

In the section marked Honorifics he almost let himself go in the fashion which I had come to recognize as typically Mencken, and which always delighted me.

> The honorifics in everyday use in England and the United States show some notable divergences. . . . In America every practitioner of any branch of the healing art is a doctor ipso facto, but in England a good many surgeons lack the title and even physicians may not have it. . . . An English dentist or druggist or veterinarian is never Dr. nor is the title frequent among pedagogues, for the Ph.D. is an uncommon degree in England.

Mencken went on to note that Professor, like Doctor, is worked much less hard in England than in the United States, and when he got around to honorary degrees, he was very close to the Mencken of the *Prejudices.*

Before the Bridge

In the United States every respectable Protestant clergyman, save perhaps a few in the Protestant Episcopal Church, is a D.D., and it is almost impossible for a man to get into the papers as a figure in anything short of felony without becoming an LL.D., but in England such honors are granted grudgingly.

Then in full Mencken fashion he added a footnote which said: "But in Scotland any clergyman over fifty, never caught red-handed in simony or adultery, is likely to be a D.D." Some honorifics in America, he added, were granted even more lightly than the D.D. degree. He quoted a traveling Scottish physician, Alexander Hamilton, who said he had found, during the mid-1700s, an immense number of colonels along the Hudson River. "It is common saying here," Hamilton wrote, "that a man has no title to that dignity unless he has killed a rattlesnake." Mencken made no comment about it, but this habit which Americans had of giving many people the title of "Colonel" has continued to this day and has even been extended in Kentucky where a man can be made a Colonel without even killing one rattlesnake.

Opposite page:

Above, H. L. Mencken when he was about fifty years old. He still had his plastered-down hair style with the part right down the middle. Courtesy: The *Baltimore Sun.*

Below, Mencken had a great sense of humor. This cartoon drawing called "The Subconscious Mencken" was made by McKee Barclay in 1912 when Mencken was thirty-two years old. Mencken had The *Sun* print it as his picture whenever the readers of his column "The Free Lance" asked to see what he looked like. Actually, Mencken was a rather handsome fellow despite his plastered-down hair style and clothes which often made him look like "a plumber on vacation," as one of his admirers said. Courtesy: The *Baltimore Sun.*

Mencken poked fun at teachers throughout most of his career and called all of them, from kindergarten to graduate school, pedagogues which he frequently shortened to "gogues." Nevertheless, in *The American Language* he usually wrote respectfully of teachers, particularly such speech and philology experts as Dr. Louise Pound of Nebraska, Dr. Kemp Malone of Johns Hopkins, and Dr. George Philip Krapf of Columbia. But he could not resist a few outbursts such as the one he delivered against English teachers.

In the American colleges and high schools, there is no faculty so weak as the English faculty. It is the common catchall for aspirants to the birch who are too lazy or too feeble in intelligence to acquire any sort of exact knowledge, and the professional incompetence of its typical ornament is matched only by his hollow cocksureness.

I had noticed in *Prejudices* and in his other writings that Mencken had attacked nearly every group in America—farmers, newspapermen, bankers, lawyers, teachers, chiropractors, politicians, and dozens of others. He usually did it in such a witty and charming manner that it never bothered me even when I was a member of the particular group under attack, but it did not surprise me when I read in the newspapers, from time to time, that some of these groups had responded in kind. Or as close to the Mencken style as they were capable of. However, it did surprise me to learn that Mencken had collected representative samples of these denunciations of himself and had published them in a book he called *Schimpflexikon*. Mencken wrote an introductory note to *Schimpflexikon* in which he said:

This collection is not exhaustive, but an effort has been made to keep it representative. The original materials would fill many volumes: they include hundreds of savage articles and newspaper editorals and a number of whole pamphlets. During the single year of 1926 more than five

The Sage of Baltimore

hundred separate editorials upon the sayings and doings of Mr. Mencken were printed in the United States and at least four-fifths of them were unfavorable. . . . There is room here only to offer some salient specimens of this anti-Mencken invective—mainly single sentences or phrases torn from their incandescent context. Some were chosen for their wit—for there are palpable hits among them!—some for their blistering ferocity, and some for their charming idiocy.

The Mencken denunciations chosen to go in *Schimpflexikon* filled 132 pages. Many of them certainly were charmingly idiotic, and nearly all of them were colorful. They came from almost every one of the forty-eight states then in the Union with selections from the South being the most numerous— probably because Mencken had belabored the South more than he had other parts of the nation.

However, the West, or that part of it which Mencken called the "hog and Bible belt," came up with some real beauties as illustrated from the following item from the *Omaha World-Herald,* which threw in Sinclair Lewis along with Mencken in its comment:

> To further the mysterious processes and purposes of life such human beings as Lewis and Mencken have their ordained place, together with the jackals and the weeds, the vermin and the microbes.

Even the sedate *Philadelphia Inquirer* got in a dig at the Sage in a brief editorial which said, in part:

> Perhaps society needs Mencken as nature needs mosquitoes. However, it will be observed that we still screen against mosquitoes."

The even more sedate William Allen White of the *Emporia Gazette* said:

Before the Bridge

With a pig's eyes which never look up, with a pig's snout that loves muck, with a pig's brain that knows only the sty, and a pig's squeal that cries only when he is hurt, he sometimes opens his pig's mouth, tusked and ugly, and lets out the voice of God, railing at the whitewash that covers the manure about his habitat.

William Randolph Hearst's *Atlanta Georgian* came up with one of the least incandescent remarks about Mencken to come from the South:

Personally, I should rather be a hillbilly of the Bible Belt than to have been born with a silver spoon in my mouth, and that spoon filled with galvanized gall.

The Jackson, Mississippi *Herald* was more typical of the southern reaction to the Sage of Baltimore. It called him "A Howling Hyena."

All of these interested me, but the two quotations which delighted me most came from Maryland, one from the Eastern Shore and the other from the western side of the Bay. "A monumental jackass, a liar supreme," the *Easton Star* said, while the *Westminster Times* said: "He must have a miserable little shriveled up soul."

And so it went for the entire 132 pages.

I did not realize in 1933 that *The American Language* had already become an American classic which probably will endure as long as the American language itself endures, nor did I know, of course, that some of Mencken's most charming works were yet to be written. His autobiographical *Days* books, for example, were easily the most delightful things he ever wrote. He denounced nothing and was simply in a mellow mood when he wrote them, but in all other respects they were typical Mencken.

Although I lived for two years just three blocks north of where Mencken and his wife had their apartment during the early 1930s, I never met him or even saw him. However, I did write him a letter and received a prompt reply. I told him that I

The Sage of Baltimore

had read in one of his books a statement to the effect that there were a dozen ways to prepare crabs, all of them giving a product superior to the best oyster dishes. I then asked him if he had ever eaten a cold freshly shucked oyster on the half-shell—an oyster taken from the salty waters in the lower part of the Chesapeake Bay, not one from the brackish water around Kent Island.

My letter was full of suggestions that Mencken was an ignorant city fellow who did not know what a really good oyster was. Mencken ignored all the suggestions and told me courteously that indeed he had eaten oysters such as I had described and they were excellent, but he still thought that many crab dishes were even better. I did not know it at the time, but it was Mencken's policy to answer all letters promptly and to give courteous answers unless the writer was insulting, obscene, and profane. In which cases he simply replied: "Dear Sir, You may be right." My letter was not in the category which demanded this reply so it was a courteous even friendly one.

As I said earlier, I began my reading assignment at Enoch Pratt Free Library thinking Mencken was a local phenomenon which I should learn more about. I finished my Mencken readings convinced that he was a great national resource, far more valuable than the Pennsylvania coal mines or the Texas oil fields and about equal to the Chesapeake Bay itself.

FIFTEEN

Epsom Salts

HAVING tasted such exciting things as big time football, championship lacrosse, the books of H. L. Mencken, and various other delights which Baltimore had offered during my first ten months there I was reluctant to see the school year end.

I knew that with the end of the school year at Brooklyn Park Junior High School would come the end of the monthly checks which had permitted me to live in Baltimore. I suspected that Mrs. Morris might be willing to carry me on the cuff for a few weeks or even all summer, but I knew that she already had more nonpaying customers at 1010 Cathedral Street than she needed.

So early in June I began to look around for a job, and the first place that came to mind was the General Chemical Company on the west side of Hanover Street near the bridge leading to Brooklyn. I had been riding past this location twice daily for nine months, but I had no idea what General Chemical manufactured, nor did I know that it really was a division of Allied Chemical Corporation, a conglomerate which had been pulled together by Eugene Meyer, father of Katherine Graham of *Washington Post* fame.

But it did not really matter to me what they made. They obviously were making chemicals of some sort, and I had, in addition to a need for money, a desire to do something more chemical than to teach general science to junior high school students who found chemistry to be a very dull subject except when something blew up.

So the Monday after school closed I presented myself to the front office of the General Chemical Company and told

Epsom Salts

them I was looking for work. Unemployment in Baltimore was still close to twenty percent, and in retrospect I realize that I had more than a normal share of optimism and naiveté. But heavy as these two ingredients were they were outweighed by my good luck.

"Skelly at the Epsom salts plant may have an opening," the man at the front office told me. "It is the third building down from here."

It turned out that Mr. Skelly (I never learned his first name) was chief supervisor of the Epsom salts factory, and when I located him and told him why I was there, he gave me a quick look, shook his head, and started to walk away, but then said abruptly:

"Are you a college graduate?"

I said that I was but added at once that I was willing to take any job available.

"I know. They all are. The big bosses at Allied have decided that now is a good time for them to hire college graduates and train them from the ground up. And because my plant is the only busy one on the site I get the privilege of training most of them."

He looked me over carefully and added: "And I can tell you some of them need a lot of training."

It was clear to me that Mr. Skelly was not really pleased to have me standing there, but since I got the impression that he had offered me a job or was about to, I asked him what I would be doing and when I would start.

"You can start tomorrow morning if you want the job," he said. "You will be an operator's helper working for Charley Hughes who is chief operator on the day shift in the Epsom salts operation. The pay is twenty-two dollars a week for an eight-hour day, five days a week. Be here promptly at 8:00 A.M. if you want the job. The Epsom salts plant is busy these days."

Since I did want the job, I was on the scene well before 8:00 A.M. on Tuesday. I could not find Skelly but found Charley Hughes and told him I was supposed to work for him. Apparently Skelly had alerted him because he said: "Okay, College Boy, we got a lot to do so let's get going." Charley never called me anything except College Boy throughout the summer. At first he said it rather derisively but later on used a clearly friendly tone.

While I certainly wanted the job I now had, I was a little shamefaced about the product we were making. Therefore, at first I did not tell my fellow roomers at 1010 Cathedral Street what my new job was.

Epsom salts were not considered to be a topic suitable for table discussion in those days when they were much more widely used than is the case today. Even then people were puzzled as to whether the name was plural or singular. However, chemists knew it was the common name for the heptahydrate of magnesium sulfate and that the name derived from the fact that magnesium sulfate was the active ingredient in the curative waters at Epsom Downs in England, one of the most famous spas in Queen Victoria's day.

During the late 1800s and early 1900s various chemical companies began to sell the long grayish white crystals of hydrated magnesium sulfate as a concentrated form of what English nobility and gentry believed help cure them of gout and other ailments caused by eating too much. At first the Epsom salts were formed by evaporating the spa waters, but that practice ended when chemists showed the product could be made more cheaply by a direct synthesis route.

The price of Epsom salts then declined sharply, and it became widely used as a hydragogue of great potency. By the 1920s it had become accepted by mothers all over the civilized world, but particularly in the United States, as a sovereign remedy for nearly all the complaints of childhood, ranging from a chest cold to indigestion caused by eating too much chocolate cake. It had only one rival in the medicine cabinet—castor oil—when I was growing up, and the children I knew were often given a choice between the two. This choice was about the same as asking a boy if he wished to be beaten with a switch or a belt strap.

Anyway, the uses of Epsom salts were too well known for me to boast about the new business I had entered. Nor was I the only one who took no pride in Baltimore's Epsom salts

Epsom Salts

plant. The Miller Brothers Restaurant was famous not only for its superb crab imperial but also for the signs painted on its walls up near the ceiling, boasting that

> Baltimore Has the Largest Straw Hat Factory
>   in America
> The World's Largest Steel Mill on a Salt Water
>   Port is Located in Baltimore
> The Largest Fertilizer Factory East of the
>   Mississippi is in Baltimore
> The First Umbrella Factory in America was
>   Built in Baltimore

Well, Baltimore also had the largest Epsom salts factory in the world at that time, but Miller Brothers Restaurant never mentioned this fact. And neither did I until I came home from my first day's work dripping with perspiration, and Mrs. Morris asked me what I was doing. So I told her I was manufacturing magnesium sulfate, hoping she would not know what it was. And apparently she did not because she gave me a puzzled look and walked on.

But Mr. LaCroix, who was standing nearby at the time, did know what it was. "Isn't magnesium sulfate the chemical name for Epsom salts?" he asked. I said that it was, and Mr. LaCroix smiled.

"You have picked a promising new field, Mr. Wingate. Nothing seems to concern Americans more than the state of their lower intestines. A friend of mine in Paris once told me that the French, English, and Americans all have national obsessions concerning different parts of their bodies. The French worry about their livers, the English about their minds, and the Americans about their bowels. I must say these national concerns seem to be justified because in each case the organ in question seldom seems to work well. Your new job is not as dignified as being a teacher but I predict you will find it a rapidly growing business."

Mr. LaCroix was one of the most remarkable of all the roomers at 1010 Cathedral Street. A Frenchman, with a snow

145

white goatee and an equally white fringe of hair above both ears, he looked like an older version of the founder of the famous Kentucky Fried Chicken chain. His wife had died years before and he lived, alone, in the third floor apartment at 1010 Cathedral Street. He was a strict vegetarian who ate only fruits, nuts, and cornflakes and milk. I liked him partly because he carried himself with great dignity under what seemed to me to be very difficult circumstances, and partly because he had once called me an authority on all scientific matters.

Mr. LaCroix had an obsession—the foraminifera—and he frequently told me about them and their many merits. I had never heard of the foraminifera until I met Mr. LaCroix, but he said they were tiny sea animals who had built up the chalk cliffs of Dover and coral islands all over the world. They had done this, he said, by living, dying, and depositing their microscopic shells on top of each other for countless thousands of years. He gave these tiny shellfish credit for great nobility of purpose and amazing devotion to their objective, and said the human race would do well to emulate them. It seemed to me that the foraminifera had no more purpose than so many molecules of salt coming out of solution to make a lump of rock salt. But I never told Mr. LaCroix this partly because he seemed to be a lonely old man who needed some heroes and partly because I had learned that he was a fierce antagonist in any argument. Some of my fellow roomers were less cautious than I was.

I came home one night during the winter to be greeted by Mrs. Morris with a merry twinkle in her eye. Two of her roomers had got in an argument with Mr. LaCroix on his favorite subject, the foraminifera, when they told him his small heroes had no more nobility of purpose than so many grains of sand being blown around the beach to make sand dunes. Mr. LaCroix was incensed by this insult to the foraminifera and ended the argument by saying: "We can refer the matter to Mr. Wingate who is a teacher and an authority on matters of science."

Having set the stage with this account of what had gone before, Mrs. Morris then left to summon Mr. LaCroix and his

Epsom Salts

two opponents to hear my decision. I sensed that her special merriment came from the fact that she already knew my private views about the foraminifera. She found Mr. LaCroix but his two opponents had gone out and so she said she and Mr. LaCroix would tell the other two what I had decided.

Given this brief interval to collect my thoughts I had not the slightest intention of betraying a man who apparently had the typical European respect for teachers and who, in addition, thought I was an authority on anything. Therefore, I gave my decision to Mr. LaCroix as soon as he came down to the living room.

It is my considered opinion as a scientist and philospher that the foraminifera have always been motivated by a sublime purpose, and their persistence over millions of years is proof of that high purpose. Their behavior is at least as noble and far more rational than that of the people who built the pyramids and led the Children's Crusade.

Mr. LaCroix beamed, and I suspect that decision was one of the reasons why he spoke encouragingly to me about my future in the Epsom salts business. However, as the summer progressed it was difficult for me to believe that I really had found a promising new field for the future.

The manufacturing of Epsom salts, as we carried it out at General Chemical in those days, was a simple but dreadful process. We dumped fourteen sacks of powdered magnesium carbonate ore into a large vat filled about half full with water. Then with the agitator in the vat going to keep this slurry in suspension, we ran concentrated sulfuric acid into the mixture thereby converting the magnesium carbonate into carbon dioxide and magnesium sulfate, the product we wanted. The addition to the acid had to be done with some care to avoid a too rapid release of carbon dioxide which would cause the slurry to foam over. After the desired reaction had taken place, it was necessary to filter the whole solution through a large iron filter press to remove the clay and other insoluble materials which were in the starting ore.

Then the clear solution from the filter press was cooled in a separate vat to cause the long gray white needles of Epsom salts to crystallize out. These needles were next filtered off in a centrifuge and dried in a rotary filter to yield the product sold in drugstores across the nation. We produced two grades of crystals, the long nearly perfect needles known to most children during the 1920s, and a grade of broken, partly dehydrated crystals which we sold to the Phillips Company for conversion to magnesium hydroxide and sold by them as Phillips Milk of Magnesia. This product had the same purpose as Epsom salts, but had a less obnoxious taste and a better general reputation.

There was a lot of heavy work in our operation but the dirtiest, most objectionable part was the cleaning of that huge iron filter press used to remove the clay and other insolubles. The chief operator on my shift, Charley Hughes, was a shrewd, wiry native of West Virginia, and since he was the boss, he naturally assigned the press job to me. This job had to be done at least once, early on the shift, and sometimes twice a day. Consequently, I was sopping wet with perspiration, steam, and dilute sulfuric acid by nine o'clock each morning, and I stayed that way all day. I also had to help Charley load the sacks of ore into the vat and I noticed that while I outweighed my boss by at least thirty pounds he hefted the sacks more easily than I did. Both of us swore at the Russian ore which we used in increasing amounts as the summer wore on, because it contained more clay than the better grade of ore and usually caused us to clean the filter press twice—once in the morning and once again in the afternoon.

During the course of the summer Charley and I became good friends, and I learned that he was a veteran of World War I, who held firmly to the opinion that the military doctors at Fort Meade would have killed him if his wife had not intervened.

"I got the flu just after we came back from France, and they sent me to Fort Meade to recover. While I was in the hospital

there, I started to go blind and deaf at the same time. I knew
that what I needed was a drink of whiskey but the damn fool
doctors wouldn't allow me to have none. Sure as hell I would
have died or at least have gone blind except for the fact that my
wife, who was working at Curtis Bay, sneaked a pint of whiskey
from down home to me at the hospital. I drank it all that night
and was out of the hospital two days later. And I ain't never
been in a hospital since then."

Charley wore a leather strap studded with strips of copper
on his right wrist and I once asked him if this strap strength-
ened his wrist. "It give me strength all over," he replied.

This was before the wearing of copper bracelets to ward
off arthritis became popular, and I do not know what gave
Charley his strength but he was a tireless worker who handled
all elements of the job with ease. He often gave me a hand with
the second cleaning of that infernal filter press and showed me
how to move the plates without causing them to get jammed
against the guide rails.

The ever-increasing demand for our product and the increased use of the Russian ore were bad enough, but by the
middle of July Baltimore began to get really hot, and I started
to sweat at 1010 Cathedral Street almost as much as I did at
work. The Freon refrigerants had been invented a couple of
years earlier, but the air conditioning industry was still in its
infancy. Even the theatres had only makeshift air conditioning
which involved blowing air over cakes of ice, and practically no
Baltimore homes were air conditioned.

The city's red brick buildings, blacktopped streets, and flat
black roofs soaked up the July sun like a sponge and released
enough heat each night to keep Baltimore steaming twenty-
four hours a day. A long period of bright sunshiny weather
began about the middle of July and by the middle of August
things were so hot that the tar in the streets was soft and sticky.
There were heel marks all over town and even the automobiles
left the imprint of their tires in the blacktop.

One day I came back to 1010 Cathedral Street so dripping
with perspiration that even the tops of my shoes were wet. Mrs.
Morris noticed this and said: "My goodness, I never knew

chemistry was such hard work."

I assured her I never knew it either, and I began to realize that I had the wrong amount of education for a career in chemistry. The Baltimore which had appealed to me so much during the previous ten months was being washed away by the rivers of sweat flowing from me night and day.

The situation reached a climax late in August. Charley and I cleaned the filter press twice that day, and I came home to find 1010 Cathedral Street about as hot as the boiler room on a Chesapeake Bay steamboat. There was a slight breeze blowing but it did not help; the moving air felt like a blast from an oven.

I sloshed around in a pool of perspiration until about four in the morning, and then concluded that it was useless to try to sleep so I got dressed and went downstairs. There I found Mr. LaCroix sitting on the white front steps eating a bowl of cornflakes. He was wearing only shoes, pants, and an undershirt and for once he had nothing to say about the foraminifera. We talked only of the weather and our hopes that a storm or something else would break the hot spell. Finally Mr. La-Croix suggested that we walk over to Mt. Vernon Square where it might be cooler because of the green grass there. When we arrived we found the grass almost entirely covered with people sleeping or trying to do so. We picked our way among them for a while and then decided to return to 1010 Cathedral Street by way of Park Avenue.

When we approached Madison Street we looked up at the tall spire of the First Presbyterian Church and saw it outlined in the soft light of early dawn, even though we could not see the sun itself. It was a lovely sight and the only pleasant thing about Baltimore I had noticed for a week. However, it was not enough to cause me to consider changing the decision I had made earlier that night.

When I went to work that day, still groggy and sweaty, I told Mr. Skelly that I wanted to quit my job at the end of the week. He said that it was okay by him, and I realized that he probably had a long list of applicants waiting to take the job I was leaving. But when I broke the news to Charley Hughes, he

Epsom Salts

gave me a friendly grin and said: "You lasted longer than I expected, College Boy."

I left Baltimore Saturday morning on the W. B. & A. train for Annapolis, in time to catch the first ferryboat to Matapeake, and while I was watching the automobiles load on the ferry, I was delighted to see that the last car was a Chevrolet convertible with the top down and Ed Evans, a fellow student at Washington College, at the wheel.

Ed and I greeted each other the way friends do when they meet unexpectedly, with back slapping and a few profane but friendly remarks.

"Where are you going?" Ed then asked me, and when I told him Cambridge, he laughed.

"So am I. I'm on my way to see Lorraine Pink. If you are not driving a car, how about riding with me?"

I said I would be delighted because if I didn't, I would have to hitchhike a ride or wait for the next Red Star bus which was not due to arrive for another three hours.

The weather changed abruptly when the ferry began to move. It was hot in Annapolis, even though not as hot as in Baltimore, but the breezes on the Chesapeake were cool and generally delightful. Even the odor was good.

Ed and I talked football most of the time, and he told me he was eager to get back to Washington College for his final football season. He said the college had a fine squad with everything required for a winning team.

"We may go undefeated," he said.

I said that would be great but not for even a second did I believe it would really happen. I remembered all too clearly the fact that we had won only two games during my four years as a student there. Amazingly, it turned out that Ed was right.

When we arrived at the new bridge across the Choptank River at Cambridge, it felt like we were back on the Chesapeake, and the twenty or thirty people who were lined up along the bridge fishing looked quite comfortable even though the sun was shining brightly. I asked Ed to drop me at

Before the Bridge

the main Phillips Packing Company complex at the south end of Cambridge Creek because I knew that Mark had been working there to raise money for his second year at Washington College. I thought he might still be there even though it was then about one o'clock in the afternoon.

The trucks and wagons loaded with tomatoes were still lined up for about half a mile waiting to unload their product, and the plant was clearly running at full blast even though it was Saturday afternoon, when most Dorchester Countians liked to quit work and go shopping in Cambridge. The man at the employment office said he knew Mark and thought he was working in the warehouse. He then went to the time card rack and pulled out a card.

"According to this card," he said, "Mark clocked in yesterday at 8:00 A.M. and is still there. Go over to the warehouse and see if he really is there or just forgot to ring out his time card when he left."

When I went to the warehouse and asked for Mark, one of the men up front said: "Sure he's here but he is sleeping right now. Let me get rid of this truck, and I'll go wake him up."

When Mark appeared I asked him if he really had been working for twenty-eight straight hours.

Mark laughed at the question.

"Sure, all of us here in the warehouse have been here since yesterday morning, and we will all get paid for twenty-eight hours because that is what the time cards will show. But everybody knows we sneak an hour or two sleep when things aren't too busy. Phillips is glad to have us here even if we do get a little sleep from time to time. They will be glad to have us as long as that half-mile line of trucks and wagons loaded with contract tomatoes is waiting out front, and they can't get enough workers to handle the rush. When we get so sleepy we just can't keep our eyes open we go back in the stack of boxes and nap for a little while. If the foreman catches someone asleep, he is required to fire him but they are always glad to hire him back the next day. In late September when a guy gets fired, they may make it stick but right now it is nothing to be worried about."

Epsom Salts

Nevertheless, Mark decided to clock out at 2:00 P.M., and we went in town to eat at Virgil's Oyster House. Virgil had no oysters then, of course, but he served us some excellent soft-shelled crabs.

Since we had no means of getting to our home at Wingate until Albert Kirwan's bus left at about 10:00 P.M., we went around to the pool hall to play a game of pool or do some bowling. The place was crowded, so we sat down on a bench to wait for a vacant table, and Mark fell asleep. Later on we went to see *The Gold Diggers of 1933*, then playing at the Arcade movie theater, and both of us fell asleep. It didn't matter because each of us had seen the show at an earlier date. We woke up when the lights went on, and the crowd started to leave.

Albert Kirwan's bus left a half an hour later and we arrived at Wingate at about eleven o'clock. There was a cool breeze blowing in from the Honga River and Fox Creek, and both of us slept until nine o'clock Sunday morning. When we got up, the breezes seemed almost as cool as they had been while crossing the Chesapeake and the Choptank a day earlier. But when we went outside to get more of these breezes, a swarm of hungry mosquitoes quickly drove us back in the house.

While August was the low point for 1934, things changed for the better in September, and my second year in Baltimore was almost as exciting as my first, even though I was careful to stay away from acetylene in the classroom. I saw Navy defeat Army in football for the first time in twelve years and played lacrosse with Mt. Washington's championship team, but I must admit that Baltimore had changed enough so that it no longer seemed like a Baghdad on the Chesapeake.

Things changed at the Epsom salts plant also, even though several years went by before I learned of them. For one thing demand for the product began to decline as business in general began to improve. A research team of medical men and sociologists may wish to study this relationship some day. But long before more sophisticated products became available to take care of what Mr. LaCroix called "the American obsession," a far more serious blow fell upon Baltimore's great Epsom salts plant. The Dow Chemical Company developed a cheaper process for making magnesium sulfate and simply drove General Chemical out of the business.

I don't know whether Charley Hughes was still working for General Chemical when this happened or had gone home to West Virginia, as he often told me he planned to do. However, if General Chemical had gone over completely to the use of Russian ore I suspect that Charley, if he was still there, welcomed the shutdown.

SIXTEEN

Celsius on Kent Island

KENT Island is the most western part of Queen Anne's County and has more saltwater shoreline per acre of land area than any other part of Maryland except the western third of nearby Talbot County. This island, which was one of the first parts of Maryland to be settled by white men, is one of the most attractive sections of the state. It is perhaps not quite as enchantingly beautiful as the Blackwater area of Dorchester County, but on the other hand, it does not have as many mosquitoes.

Wide expanses of salt water—Eastern Bay, the broad mouth of the Chester River, and Chesapeake Bay itself—surround Kent Island on three sides, but it is bounded on the fourth side by Kent Narrows, a body of water so narrow that many people ride over the bridge across it without being aware of its existence. To these people Kent Island is merely a peninsula sticking out into Chesapeake Bay, thereby permitting the bridge from the Eastern Shore to Anne Arundel County on the western shore to be several miles shorter than it otherwise would have been. Kent Island also permitted the ferryboat routes, which preceded the Bay Bridge, to be shorter than they otherwise would have been. Before the days of the bridge and the ferries Kent Island was almost as isolated as Hooper Island or even Tangier Island.

Today Kent Island is a major center for the seafood industry and a prime residential area because of that vast shoreline already mentioned, but ever since 1935 whenever I think of it, I also think of the metric system of weights and measures and Anders Celsius.

Before the Bridge

During the past century or so the United States government and many American scientific organizations have made determined efforts to have the metric system replace the English system of weights and measures in this country. They point out that grams and kilograms, degrees Celsius, and meters and kilometers are a far more convenient way of measuring things than ounces and pounds, degrees Fahrenheit, and yards and miles. As a part of this selling job the weather programs on TV often report the temperature in both degrees Fahrenheit and degrees Celsius, while some states have road markers which give distances in kilometers as well as miles. All this is done in the hope that some day the metric system will cause Americans to forget all about inches, miles, degrees Fahrenheit, and such things while speaking only of grams, meters, and degrees Celsius. However, if there has been any real progress in that direction it has come slowly—inch by inch, so to speak, and not in kilometers.

I believe my own experience on Kent Island, during the winter of 1935, helps explain why progress has been so slow. Late in January of that year a classmate of mine at Crapo High School, Emory Coughlin, invited me to drive with him from Baltimore to our home territory in south Dorchester County, and I accepted with alacrity. I was homesick for the taste of oysters from Tangier Sound and I hoped my father would have a supply on hand even though the very cold weather had iced over many of the oyster grounds farther up the Bay.

Just when the cooling system in Emory's automobile froze I do not know, but it probably was during the ferryboat trip from Baltimore to Love Point, the most northern tip of Kent Island. We sat in a heated section of the ferry during the hour and a half trip across the upper part of the Chesapeake, but we saw that ice was already starting to pile up in sections of the Bay even though we had no trouble cutting through the frozen parts which lay along our route. In any event, we had driven only a few miles from Love Point when we saw the telltale puffs of steam coming from under the hood of our car and realized that we would never make it to Dorchester County with a frozen radiator and no circulation to cool the motor. So when

Celsius on Kent Island

we saw a garage-filling station just before we reached the Kent Narrows Bridge, we pulled in to ask for help.

The garage was a small one, big enough to hold two or three cars, but clearly not designed for the kind of weather we were having that day. There was no door on the main entrance but inside the area covered by the roof we saw a man stretched out on his back on a dolly under the car he was working on, while over in a corner, away from the entrance, was a pot-bellied coal stove with two men seated on a bench near it.

It must have been obvious to all what our problem was, and one of the two men seated near the stove defined it succinctly. "She's all froze up," he said.

The man on the dolly pushed himself out from under the car he was working on and told us to pull our car in as close as we could to the stove. "After the radiator warms up some," he said, "I'll put in a couple of quarts of antifreeze and you can be on your way." Emory did as instructed, and we then joined the two men seated by the stove to wait for the radiator to thaw out and to get warm ourselves. After a few moments of silence one of the men seated there, a fellow wearing felt-lined knee-length rubber boots, spoke up. "It's colder than hell out there," he said, "but I've seen it colder."

This comment seemed to be only a friendly remark designed to make Emory and me feel at home, but the other man seated there, a younger man wearing a waist-length coat with a hunting license on the back, promptly challenged it.

"No you ain't. It's zero on the thermometer, and it just cain't get no colder than that."

"You are wrong about that. I've seen it twice as cold as it is today. In fact, if the wind was blowing, it would be twice as cold right now."

"The wind ain't got nothing to do with how cold it is. Besides that, twice zero is still zero. I tell you it cain't get no colder than it is today."

"It sure can. Like I told you it is always twice as cold when the wind is blowing, and it's twice as cold as that if you are out on the water."

Before the Bridge

The conversation might have ended in a draw at that point except for the fact that Emory, who had just completed his studies in civil engineering at Johns Hopkins University, decided to enter the discussion. "It is possible," he said to the younger man, "for the temperature to fall below zero. As a matter of fact it is colder than zero in many parts of the world right now. Also, on the Celsius thermometer, it is eighteen degrees below zero right here on Kent Island." There was a brief pause and then the younger man spoke again.

"I don't see where Celsius, or whatever you call it, has anything to do with how cold it is. The thermometer said it was zero this morning when I looked at it and it ain't got no colder since then. And I tell you it cain't get no colder."

"Not all thermometers use the same scale," Emory replied. "Water freezes at thirty-two degrees on the Fahrenheit scale, but it doesn't freeze until zero on the Celsius thermometer. When it is zero Fahrenheit, it is nearly eighteen degrees below zero Celsius." This information caused the man in the felt boots to speak up again.

"You mean to say," he asked, "that you have two thermometers which are thirty-two degrees apart in one direction and only eighteen apart the other way? That's like saying it is seven miles from here to Queenstown and only four from Queenstown to here."

Emory began to look from side to side, like a man searching for help or at least a way out of the situation. Then he apparently decided to plunge ahead.

"No, that is not really what I was saying. You can use a whole lot of scales in making thermometers. On the Kelvin or Absolute scale water freezes at 273 degrees above zero, but when you get to Absolute zero it can't get any colder."

"See," the younger man said vigorously, "I told you, you cain't get no colder than zero."

"I guess I didn't make myself clear," Emory replied. "You can get colder than zero Celsius or even zero Fahrenheit but you can't get colder than zero Absolute. There is still heat in a cake of ice at zero Fahrenheit but not at zero Absolute."

Celsius on Kent Island

"Well, it was absolutely zero this morning," the younger man came back, "and I still say it cain't get no colder than that."

"There is a difference between absolutely zero and Absolute zero," Emory said. "It really can't get any colder than Absolute zero."

"Yes it can if the wind is blowing," the older man said. "It will be twice as cold just like I said."

"No," Emory said patiently, "when it is minus 273 on the Celsius thermometer, it is as cold as it can get whether the wind is blowing or not."

The older man looked at Emory carefully for a few seconds.

"You mean to tell me that it can get to 273 below zero, but it can't get to 283 below, or even 275 below, no matter what happens?"

Emory was still thinking about a reply to that question when the man asked another one.

"When it is 273 degrees below zero on your Celsius thermometer, what temperature is it on a real thermometer?"

An anguished look crossed Emory's face, but he answered truthfully.

"If by a real thermometer you mean a Fahrenheit thermometer, I'm not exactly sure, but I think it is about 450 degrees below zero."

"I knew it could get colder than 273 degrees below zero if it really wanted to," the older man said, "but you said just a little while ago that it couldn't."

"I did," Emory replied, "but it all depends on what system you are using. It really can't get below zero on the Absolute scale."

"That's what I been telling both of you," the younger man said.

There was silence for several moments, and then the booted man moved in on Emory again.

"Did you say back there a little while ago," he asked "that there is heat in a cake of ice?"

"Yes I did," Emory replied. "There is heat in a cake of ice if it is at zero Celsius or even zero Fahrenheit but not at zero Absolute."

The older man slowly shook his head, looked at the younger fellow, shrugged, and never said anything further.

However, the younger man decided to have one last word.

"There is too many people messing around with the weather. If they keep it up it's likely to stay so cold that a man won't be able to go arstering for the rest of the winter."

I had been aware, all through this discussion, that at 40 degrees below zero it doesn't make any difference whether you use a Celsius or Fahrenheit scale. The reading is the same on both thermometers, and I had been planning to drop this information into the discussion at some point. But with the older man apparently convinced that Emory was some kind of a nut, and the younger man convinced that too many people were messing with the weather I decided to keep quiet. The conversation ended and it seemed to me that Celsius was probably never going to be accepted on Kent Island.

But you never can tell. After our radiator thawed out and the garage owner tightened a hose fitting and put in two quarts of antifreeze, Emory and I started to leave. When we did, the garage owner turned his back toward the two men near the stove, nodded ever so slightly over his shoulder at them, grinned, and winked broadly at Emory and me.

Today Celsius readings probably cause no problem for most of the people living on Kent Island. Certainly it is no problem for one of the Chesapeake Bay's most distinguished scientists, Dr. Reginald Van Trump Truitt, who now makes his home there.

SEVENTEEN

Muskrat Gloves and Oysters

DURING the spring of 1938 Vic and I went home for a visit and on our way back to Baltimore decided to inspect the new Blackwater Wildlife Refuge. We were not attracted by the scenic beauty of the area, which we both knew well, but by a desire to see the big new muskrats, called nutria, which had recently been imported from South America and were being tested to see if they liked the environment in Dorchester County.

The area in and around the refuge surely is one of the most beautiful places along the Chesapeake Bay. The three winding rivers which come together there—the Blackwater, Transquaking, and Chicamacomico—move so slowly that a stranger looking at them could not be certain that they are rivers; the wider parts of each could easily be mistaken for lakes. This is particularly true of the Blackwater River where sections of it are so wide and still that the surface has a glassy look. But whatever they are, the scenery along them is enchantingly beautiful.

Lonely stands of loblolly pines, clusters of cattail, and tall phragmites break up the level symmetry of the vast stretches of low green marsh grass which can be seen in all directions. All these combine with the multitude of small lakes, creeks, and rivers to delight the human eye and make muskrats, geese, ducks, terrapin, and mosquitoes feel more at home there than in any other place in Maryland. This is the area which Aubrey Bodine, the artist with a camera, had in mind when he said that Dorchester County was easily the most scenically beautiful part of Maryland.

Before the Bridge

Although Vic and I knew the general area well, we drove around the new roads through it for five or ten minutes before we found the small headquarters building. The young biologist in charge that day said he was from Nebraska and obviously delighted with his new job; he was eager to show us the nutria when we told him what we had come to see.

"We have turned a dozen or so pairs of nutria loose in the marshes, and I think they are adjusting well, at least it seems that way because I have not seen any dead ones and I do see some live ones from time to time as I travel through the marshes. If you want to see a nutria up close, come over here to the compound where we have some which we are holding back until we see how the first ones released are getting along."

He led us to an enclosed area surrounded by fine chicken wire and said: "Wait here until I go get my muskrat gloves so I can pull one out from his hiding place."

While we were waiting for the biologist to return, one of the nutria came out of a hole in a pile of marsh grass in one corner of the compound and slowly walked over to another pile of marsh grass. He seemed not at all bothered by his human visitors and even briefly looked us in the eye. In just about every respect the nutria seemed to be an overgrown muskrat, scaled up by a factor of three or four. The nutria was still in view when the biologist returned holding a pair of gloves in his hand.

"These are special muskrat gloves," he explained, "designed and developed by Dr. Truitt of the Chesapeake Biological Laboratory at Solomons Island for protection against bites when we have to handle muskrats. Notice the thick padding on the top of each finger and the long stiff shield which goes well up past the wrist. The nutria have even longer teeth than muskrats but so far these gloves have given us perfect protection."

Vic and I took one look at the gloves and then at each other. We could scarcely hold back the laughter which was threatening to engulf both of us, because we instantly recognized these muskrat gloves as ordinary lacrosse gloves which

162

both of us had worn when we played lacrosse at the University of Maryland and Washington College.

As soon as the young biologist left us to go back to his office, Vic turned to me and said: "I know just how much time Dr. Truitt spent designing and developing those special muskrat gloves. He got on the phone to College Park and asked Jack Faber to send him half a dozen pairs of lacrosse gloves, and the job was all done."

The Dr. Truitt to whom Vic and the young biologist referred was Dr. Reginald Van Trump Truitt, the University of Maryland's first lacrosse coach, and the Jack Faber Vic mentioned was the man who succeeded Dr. Truitt as head coach of lacrosse, Dr. John E. Faber, professor of bacteriology at College Park, when Dr. Truitt left to become head of the Solomons Island Chesapeake Biological Laboratory.

While Vic knew Dr. Truitt well, I had met him for the first time in 1934 when Wilson introduced me to him at a lacrosse game at Homewood Field in Baltimore. He was a tall athletic-looking man in 1934 and amazingly he looked that same way throughout the many times I saw him during the next forty-five years.

After Wilson introduced me to him in 1934, the two of them talked for several minutes about the future of the game of lacrosse. Both of them agreed that the new rules adopted in 1933, reducing the length of the playing field and cutting the number of players on a team from twelve to ten, would probably make the game more popular with spectators, but both were apprehensive that midfield play might become less important. Dr. Truitt asked Wilson what he thought about the prospects for lacrosse in the 1936 Olympic Games, and when Wilson said he thought the prospects were not good, Dr. Truitt said: "That's too bad because Jack Faber probably is going to have a championship team at College Park that year. His sophomores should be ready then."

After Dr. Truitt left, Wilson turned to me and remarked: "There goes the man who is almost certainly the world's greatest authority on *Crassostrea virginica*."

Before the Bridge

"On what?"

"On *Crassostrea virginica*," Wilson said with the half-smile, half-grin which he often used when he was trying to teach me something.

"That's an oyster to you," he went on. "It literally means a hard-shelled native of Virginia, and I really think the oyster should have been called *Crassostrea marylandia* because there are more oysters caught in Maryland's part of the Chesapeake Bay than in Virginia's, but it was named a long time ago and nothing can be done about it now. Getting back to Truitt, he is a most unusual man. He probably knows more about the entire Chesapeake Bay than any other man alive. There may be a lot of oyster boat captains who know as much about the winds, tides, and sandbars as he does, but I'm talking about what goes on down under the surface of the water. His laboratory at Solomons Island is the first of its kind ever established anywhere along the Atlantic Coast or the Gulf of Mexico, and it is doing great work.

"When I went down to College Park to talk to him about his lacrosse team one day five or six years ago we got to discussing oysters, and he told me more about how they feed and reproduce than I had believed was known by anyone. Truitt not only knows what has been discovered over here about oysters but he apparently has read every paper which the French and English have written on the subject. He told me that more rumors and misinformation have been published about the way oysters reproduce than has been written about even the sex lives of Charlie Chaplin, Fatty Arbuckle, Rudolph Valentino, and all the other movie stars combined. He also told me that Curley Byrd knows a lot about oysters too but not as much as he thinks he knows and that Curley's father is more of an oyster expert than Curley is. However, no one can question Truitt's knowledge of oysters. It is amazing. When we were talking about oysters he was quoting everyone from the old Roman, Pliny, to the French scientist, Coste, who worked on oysters for Napoleon III for a quarter of a century, but his own studies at Solomons Island have put him far ahead of Coste.

Muskrat Gloves and Oysters

Since we had that first conversation, he has sent me three or four papers which he has written himself or received from some other source. If he keeps it up, I may become an oyster expert myself."

My own interest in oysters was limited to finding out where the tastiest ones were caught, and I believed I already knew that so I did not pursue the subject any further at that time. But shortly before Christmas when I stopped by Wilson's house to have dinner with him and his wife Pat, he returned to the subject of oysters himself.

"Here is the latest brochure from your friend Dr. Truitt," he said, handing me a fifteen- or twenty-page booklet in mimeograph form. I passed over the comment about Dr. Truitt being my friend since both of us were aware that Wilson knew Dr. Truitt far better than I did, but I picked up the brochure and began to skim through it.

It was titled simply *The Chesapeake Bay* and apparently had been written for the benefit of the Maryland State Legislature because the basic theme of it was to the effect that Maryland should be spending more money to gain scientific knowledge about the Bay.

Under the subheading of Oysters Dr. Truitt had assembled a mass of data and calculations showing that an acre of oyster rock, under the waters of the Bay, would produce, annually, several times as many pounds of high quality protein as an acre of the most fertile soil in Carroll or Frederick counties when the farm lands in these prime agricultural areas were devoted to the growing of beef or milk. Then he said that while the state was spending large sums of money to learn how farming could be made more efficient and productive it was spending practically nothing to learn how to farm the Bay more efficiently or even how to prevent it from deteriorating from its current level of productivity. The great ignorance which the human race displayed on the care and feeding of oysters, he said, would surely some day lead to a catastrophe in the state's most valuable seafood crop. He cited the fact that France, with a much smaller potential for oyster production,

165

had been spending large sums for scientific study of oysters in their estuary areas. These studies, he said, had permitted the French to restore the Bay of Arcachon, which had been destroyed as an oyster growing area during the 1700s, to a productivity such that this tiny body of water, less than a hundredth the size of the Chesapeake Bay, was then producing half a million bushels of oysters per year. These studies had also permitted the Bay of Arcachon to recover from its oyster blight of the 1920s. We could learn valuable things from the French studies, he said, but we had to keep in mind that Chesapeake Bay oysters were a different species from those growing in French waters and the French had no body of water which came reasonably close to the Chesapeake Bay in such complex matters as variations in acidity, salinity, and diatomic life.

The main emphasis of the paper was on oysters, but it also pointed out that any scientific information concerning the Chesapeake Bay itself and the waters flowing into it would almost certainly be useful in future efforts to protect and expand the crab and fish industries. However, the thing about this paper which struck me most forcibly was its claim that the marshes which are found along the Chesapeake, particularly on the Eastern Shore, were an essential part of the Bay. Without these marshes, Dr. Truitt explained, the Chesapeake Bay probably would not be so hospitable to the many forms of life which flourish there. The living and decaying vegetation in these marshes provides food for a host of microscopic forms of life which are the first steps in a protein chain that finally produces such magnificent foods as crabs, oysters, shad, striped bass or rockfish, and black duck. The marshes themselves are economically important for such things as muskrats and diamondback terrapin, but their real importance lies in the fact that they are an essential link in the entire scheme of things for the Chesapeake Bay. The fact that dozens of fish species, such as the striped bass, perch, croaker, and herring are hatched far up in the marshes near the head of the many creeks and rivers flowing into the Chesapeake is convincing proof of the importance of the marshes. Without the marshes to feed the baby fish the large fish would soon disappear from the Chesapeake or at best become very scarce.

And yet, he concluded, ignorance about the marshes was even more nearly abysmal than it was concerning the Bay itself. This analysis of the marshes caught my attention for two reasons. First, I had been led to believe when I was living in Dorchester that the marshes were good for nothing except muskrats, which were not very important to most people, and, secondly, mosquitoes, which were nothing but a nuisance or a plague to the entire human race.

Dr. Truitt closed his paper by saying that the venture started a few years ago to grow muskrats on a muskrat farm along the Blackwater River had failed primarily because of ignorance. The people who had spent their money to start the farm simply did not know enough about the marshes and muskrats to make the venture as successful as some mink and fox farms had been in other parts of the country. He gave no details on the failure of this muskrat venture, but I wished that he had because it had intrigued me greatly during the brief time I saw it trying to operate.

The venture had been financed by money from outside Maryland, and if an analysis of its failure was ever given to its stockholders, this analysis never surfaced in Dorchester County. However, it created a lot of excitement when construction of the "muskrat farm" began just south of the Blackwater River bridge in 1925.

The owners of the farm purchased a square mile of prime muskrat marsh just east of the highway leading from Golden Hill to Church Creek and proceeded to fence it in with galvanized wire. The land probably was purchased fairly cheaply, but the fencing operation was an expensive one. The wire netting was buried to a depth of several feet, deep enough so that the muskrats were not expected to dig their way to freedom under it, and it extended up above the top of the marsh grass by a foot or so. The last ten inches were a solid strip instead of wire netting so that the captive muskrats could not pull themselves out over the top. The rumor was that soon this square mile of marsh would have a muskrat population in

Before the Bridge

excess of all the other marshes on the Eastern Shore, because the owners would provide ample food for all occupants of this muskrat metropolis.

Unfortunately for the investors it did not turn out that way. When a census of muskrat population was taken at the end of the first year, it was discovered that, so far as could be determined, there were fewer muskrats inside the galvanized enclosure than had been counted at the beginning of the operation. Whether they dug under the wire or climbed over the top or simply died from the frustration involved, no one ever was sure. Anyway, the venture was abandoned at the end of the second year and within ten years every trace of that expensive fence had rusted away and vanished.

I once asked Captain Will Dean, owner of the oyster and crab house in Toddville, if he knew what had caused the muskrat farm to be such a complete failure.

"Nobody ever told me, but I have my own theory. Them muskrats were smart enough to figure that if they were penned up there was no good end in store for them. So they spent all their time figuring how to get out instead of producing little muskrats the way they do in the open marshes."

"But they had a square mile to roam around in and all the corn and wheat they could eat provided free to them," I continued, "so I wouldn't think the muskrats would even know they were in captivity."

"That's the trouble with people like you. You don't think like a muskrat does. For all you know a muskrat might ramble over ten or fifteen miles of territory every night and when that fence held 'em back, it probably drove 'em all crazy. I understand they never even bothered the corn which the keepers put inside the fence to feed 'em."

I saw Dr. Truitt many times after I read that brochure on the Chesapeake Bay—at Maryland homecoming football games, boat races on the Choptank and Miles rivers, and other places—but I never got around to asking him just what kind of ignorance caused the muskrat farm failure until 1981, shortly before he received the Rachel Carson Award for his contributions to the ecology of the Bay.

Muskrat Gloves and Oysters

He was then ninety years old but still had the erect posture and trim figure which I had first observed in 1934. His appearance, when he came down the stairs to have lunch with me and Mrs. Truitt, the former Mary Harrington, reminded me of the homecoming football game at College Park in 1966 when Dr. Joseph Lann and his wife, Ruth, were also present.

Joe Lann had been one of Dr. Truitt's "cheap labor" assistants at the Solomons Laboratory during his undergraduate days at College Park and enjoyed the experience immensely— particularly his work with *Callinectes sapidus,* the Chesapeake Bay blue crab. Joe introduced Ruth to Dr. Truitt, and she was amazed that the Truitt figure, at age seventy-five, was the same as Joe had described it when Dr. Truitt was forty-five.

"Dr. Truitt," Ruth exclaimed, "how do you manage to maintain such a youthful figure?"

"I owe it all, madam," he replied instantly, "to piety during my youth."

I said nothing about his youthful figure in 1981, but I did finally get around to the failure of the muskrat farm on the Blackwater River.

"Dr. Truitt, do you remember the muskrat farm along the Blackwater in 1926?"

"I certainly do. I was technical advisor to the company, and I told them from the beginning that they didn't know enough about muskrats to make the thing successful. They assumed that muskrats would love to eat corn or wheat, like ordinary rats do, but they were wrong. The only thing the muskrats wanted to eat was the root of the three-square marsh grass. And even if the muskrats had been willing to breed, which they apparently were not, there would not be enough three-square grass inside that enclosure to feed the kind of rat population those people had in mind. I told them they should have started to study muskrats fifteen or twenty years before they fenced in their farm."

"Captain Will Dean told me," I said, "that the muskrats were just too smart to breed in captivity. He said the fence took away their appetite for both food and sex."

"He may be right," Dr. Truitt replied. "We don't understand muskrat psychology any better than we do human psychology. Muskrats may be the smarter of the two species."

And no one is really sure just why one man stands straight at ninety while another is all stooped over at sixty-five. It may be that a sense of humor is just as important to longevity as youthful piety.

Opposite page:

Above, Dr. Reginald V. Truitt, *top left,* coached the first University of Maryland lacrosse team to win a national championship. Others in the picture, *left to right,* are: Cecil Branner, E. F. Zalesak, H. R. Heidelbach, T. B. Marden, Gomer Lewis, and Taylor Rowe. The bottom row, *left to right,* shows: Charles "Mac" Brewer, A. R. Sleasman, Ed Smith, Ivan Marty, A. D. Osborne, Tony Hough, and Joe Burger.

Below, forty-four years later the national championship team of 1924 presented a trophy to their seventy-eight-year-old coach. Dr. Truitt was no novice in the use of lacrosse gloves when, in 1938, he recommended that they be used in handling muskrats and nutrias.

EIGHTEEN

A Motley Crew

MY last two years in the Anne Arundel County school system were spent as a teacher of mathematics and chemistry at Glen Burnie Senior High School. These two years, on balance, were even more pleasant than the previous four years at Brooklyn Park Junior High.

During those first four years, while I lived in Baltimore, some of the sheen and glitter of city life had rubbed away so that when I was transferred to Glen Burnie High, I moved out of Baltimore to Glen Burnie, then a town of some two thousand people about ten miles south of Baltimore along a rattletrap electric railroad called the W. B. & A. By the time I got to know the W. B. & A. well its name could have been shortened to B. & A. because its Washington route had been abandoned and the cars ran only between Baltimore and Annapolis.

In Glen Burnie I found room and board for twenty-eight dollars per month, with the Long family whose house was only a hundred yards or so from the school building. Garner Klair, who also taught at Glen Burnie High, had a room right across the hall from mine, while Mrs. Long, her husband, and six-year-old son Tommy filled up the other two bedrooms.

Mrs. Long fed her household in a royal manner and always urged Klair and me to have second helpings, which we often did. Tommy, however, was Mrs. Long's greatest concern at the dinner table. No matter how much he ate she always urged him to eat more. This constant pressure had the result which might be expected; Tommy played a game with his mother and the more she urged him to eat the more he resisted. This did not mean that he ever went hungry or was undernourished. He was a healthy, vigorous specimen of boyhood who

A Motley Crew

ate before dinner, after dinner, and even at dinner on certain occasions. Mr. Long watched this eating battle between his wife and his son with amused good humor and even agreed to take Tommy to see a diet specialist when Mrs. Long became particularly upset one week. The doctor told the Longs that Tommy was a healthy, normal boy who would eat enough when he got hungry.

"This," Mr. Long told Klair and me, "is what I have been saying for a year or two, but she wouldn't listen to me. Maybe I should have charged her ten dollars too, and she would have listened to me."

But Mrs. Long did not pay much attention to the expensive medical advice until one evening about two weeks later. She had baked two chickens for the five of us, and Tommy proceeded to eat all four of the drumsticks. Quite understandably, he had room for nothing else, and so he ignored the vegetables his mother had heaped on his plate. He even refused the slice of blackberry pie which she offered to him.

Whereupon Mrs. Long exclaimed: "Look at poor Tommy's plate. He hasn't eaten a thing—except those four chicken legs."

This was too much for both Klair and me, and we roared with laughter. Mrs. Long looked at us in amazement, at first, and then even she smiled at what she had said.

"Why don't you guys do that more often?" Mr. Long told us later. "You did a lot more good than that high priced doctor did."

There were many other reasons, in addition to good food, why my two years in Glen Burnie were so pleasant, and one of them was that Glen Burnie High was a large school with many fascinating characters in both the faculty and the student body. There were enough men teachers about my own age to permit us to have a faculty basketball team, which one of our witty seniors, Reid Sykes, promptly gave the nickname the Polecats.

All of Glen Burnie High's athletic teams were called the Bisons but that name did not excite the students anywhere near as much as the Polecats did. The name which Sykes gave us suggested that we stunk but such was not the case. We not only defeated the Bisons varsity team in an exhibition game which packed the gymnasium with students cheering against us, but we won every game on our schedule. True enough, this schedule did not include the Boston Celtics or the Philadelphia Sixers. Aside from the game with the Bisons we played only other high school faculty teams in Anne Arundel and Howard counties, but an undefeated team is an undefeated team. Even the students finally forgave us for beating the Bisons and the 1939 student yearbook, *Le Souvenir,* devoted an entire page to the Polecat basketball team and listed the full squad: G. Klair, G. Cullen, E. S. Zimmerman, D. Rankin, P. Harris, M. Wingate, and P. Wingate.

In a cartoon on the page of *Le Souvenir* devoted to the Polecats I was shown as captain of the team, but that is not the way it really was. The editors of the yearbook—Charles Stoll, Rudolph Parks, Charles Reilly, Reid Sykes, Lucille Gischell, Lillian Miller, and others—were all friends of mine, some going all the way back to junior high, and like all other historians before and since then, they did not hesitate to twist the facts to suit their own ideas of how things should have been. They had already dedicated the yearbook to me, and decided to make me captain of the Polecats also. Actually, the Polecats had no captain, but if one had been chosen it probably would have been Garner Klair, our best player, or Gordon Cullen, our tall center who was also famous for his tall stories.

When Cullen told a story, he nearly always embellished it so much that it sounded like Mark Twain's account of steamboats running aground on alligators in the Mississippi, or James Thurber telling about the night the bed fell on his father. When Cullen spoke about his college days, there was no one present who could challenge him, except when he claimed he had tackled Red Grange and Clark Hinkle on the same day. But when he spoke of recent happenings, he often embarrassed his young wife, Min, who frequently felt compelled to pull in the reins on him by saying: "Now, Gord—."

She never was required to finish that sentence because Cullen would then grin and say: "Now, Min, you know there is

The Polecats. Glen Burnie High School Faculty Basketball Team, *left to right*: Gordon Cullen, Edwin Zimmerman, Phil Wingate, Donald Rankin, Garner Klair. Not shown are Paul Harris and Mark Wingate, brother of the author of this book. While P. Wingate is shown as captain, he really was not.

no sense in telling a story unless you make it a good one."

In addition to the extracurricular activities at Glen Burnie High, I also enjoyed the teaching assignments more than I had at Brooklyn Park because the subject matter was more advanced than first year algebra and general science.

The principal of Glen Burnie High in those days was L. Tod Motley, and that name never failed to mislead those who saw it for the first time. L. Tod Motley was really Louisa T. Motley until she concluded that she commanded more attention and respect from strangers she corresponded with when she signed her name in such a way that these strangers believed she was a man. And without a doubt she was right because sexist prejudice was not something discovered in recent years. However, it should be noted that the Superintendent of Schools in Anne Arundel County, George Fox, did not suffer from it since he had made principals of the first two bosses I had after graduating from college—Mrs. James S. Bourke, at Brooklyn Park, and Louisa T. Motley at Glen Burnie.

Anyway, no matter how she signed her name, L. Tod Motley was distinctly feminine. She had a soft looking face and a pink complexion which had stayed with her for the fifty some years she had lived when I first met her. Her voice was as soft as her southern upbringing would suggest it should be. She also had a soft handshake and while she wore no velvet glove, she could produce a fist of steel when circumstances forced her to do so.

L. Tod was a good executive. She ran a large faculty and student body with a minimum of strain and anxiety on her part and had an organization chart which would have pleased any good military man.

At the beginning of my second year at Glen Burnie she appointed me chairman of the mathematics department, and while this exalted rank did not add a single dollar to my annual pay of one thousand six hundred dollars, Miss Motley made it clear that the position carried certain responsibilities. One of these responsibilities, she said, was to introduce some new courses which would "enrich the curriculum," something which the State Department of Education had instructed her

A Motley Crew

to do. I though about this for a few days and then suggested that we offer a course in surveying.

L. Tod, as everyone called her behind her back, looked mildly quizzical, when I made this suggestion.

"Who could teach it?"

"I could."

Whereupon she said, without further questions or comments: "Go ahead."

Surveying was great fun at Glen Burnie. We borrowed a surveyor's transit from a local contractor and carried out two projects during the one semester that the course lasted. First, we surveyed the school grounds and came within a quarter of an acre of finding the same area which the school board said we owned. Herb Linthicum, who was a star surveyor, said the school board must have done a good job in arriving at a figure as close to the truth as they did.

Herb also had some fun on our second project which was to run a line of levels from the cornerstone of the high school to another stone marker down by the Johnson Lumber Company, a half mile in toward the center of Glen Burnie. We had no independent source of information as to what this drop in elevation was so we concluded that our answer was exactly right and everyone received an A for this particular project. One term which we used often in running the line of levels was a "Turning Point" which I said surveyors usually called a "T.P." This delighted Herb who never failed to stick one hand above his head and do a brief Indian dance whenever someone said T.P.

My last year at Glen Burnie I also taught a class in "practical chemistry" which was neither practical nor chemical. We made soap from waste fats and caustic potash extracted from oak ashes and while this technology would have been highly practical back in colonial days when our ancestors did it that way, by 1939 both Lever Brothers and Procter and Gamble, which had plants in nearby South Baltimore, had left us far behind in both costs and quality. The soap we made had such an excess of alkali in it that I was forced to scrap it promptly.

The one project in practical chemistry which appeared to

interest all the students was the rum experiment. In this project we took some molasses, diluted it with water, added some yeast, and put the mixture in the furnace room for four days to permit it to ferment. After that we put the whole mass in a small glass still with a short column and distilled off forty or fifty milliliters. Everyone came to attention when I put a match to this condensate and it began to burn with a blue flame.

"It is really rum," I said, and that created a mild sensation. Everyone wanted to taste it, but I feared such a performance might get me in trouble with Miss Motley or even the school board so I told the class that we would let Carl Waldman, the largest student present, be official taster for the project. I poured out a tablespoonful of the rum, and Carl proceeded to do his duty.

"That's the best rum I ever tasted," Carl declared and I suspect that he was right, because it probably was the only rum he had ever tasted.

All in all, my last year at Glen Burnie was a great one—not only for me but for nearly all of the students and faculty members as well. We had no riots, no one walked up the down staircase, and some of the students even got a good high school education.

Much of the credit for this stellar academic performance must be given to L. Tod Motley who was, as I said earlier, a good executive. Two of the characteristics of a good executive are the ability to handle new and unusual problems and the ability to remain calm when others get excited. Miss Motley had these two abilities in good measure as she proved at the time of the famous bad word.

There aren't many bad words left today, but in those days there were a lot of them and the one referred to here was by far the worst of them all. To most Americans it is as objectionable as the word bloody is to a well-bred Englishman. It is such a bad word that even *Webster's Third New International Dictionary*, which listed all the other four-letter words, failed to include this one. Nevertheless, the word is much used today, just as it was much used in 1939, and one day someone wrote it in

A Motley Crew

the chalk dust on a desk just in front of a teacher's desk. And there it was, plain as a large wart on the nose, when the woman teacher in charge of this homeroom came in to work one morning.

This woman was a genteel sort, and the word infuriated her. She asked the handful of students who had already arrived if they knew who had written it. They said no and her fury increased. So she dispatched one of the students to Miss Motley's office to tell the principal that an emergency had arisen in Room 202 which required her presence.

Word about the situation spread like a brush fire, and when Miss Motley arrived on the scene, there were fifteen or twenty students and teachers assembled there waiting to see how she would handle this great problem.

L. Tod entered the room with all the serenity and majesty of the Queen Mother walking into an English garden to have a cup of tea. When she reached the teacher's desk, she spoke quietly.

"What is the problem?"

"Look at that," said the indignant teacher pointing to the four-letter word engraved in the chalk dust. Miss Motley did as directed, but no trace of alarm or concern was reflected on her untroubled brow.

"What does it mean?" she asked.

This question surprised her audience as much as it would have been surprised if she had broken into a dance step and shouted Hurrah! There was a stunned silence which lasted perhaps ten seconds, by which time it was clear that no one was going to answer her question or even pronounce the word.

"Well, then," she said, "if no one knows what it means, let's clean off the desk top and go back to work."

A student moved quickly to do as she had suggested, and without another word she turned and left the room. The crisis had vanished.

In retrospect it seems incredible that Miss Motley had finished four years of college and spent twenty-five years in the public schools of Maryland without ever having seen or heard of this infamous word. So perhaps she was acting, but if so it was a performance which would have done credit to Sarah Bernhardt.

Mrs. Bourke, I believe, would have handled the crisis differently. With her quick darting eyes and instant comprehension she would have sized up the whole situation the moment she entered the room and on her way to the teacher's desk would have accidentally dragged her gloves across the offending word, making it illegible to all. And without a corpus delecti there would have been no reason to seek an indictment of anyone. Mr. Fox, I am convinced, was a real expert in choosing executives for his schools.

In any event, Glen Burnie High School was a delightful place, filled with many charming people and I probably never would have left there except for three reasons: (1) the pay was low, (2) I still longed to be a practicing chemist, and (3) Dr. Charles E. White of the University of Maryland chemistry department offered me a full-time job as a laboratory instructor.

Dr. White was on the committee which reviewed my thesis for a master's degree at Maryland in the spring of 1939, and the next time he saw me he asked if I planned to go on to obtain a Ph.D. I said I did.

"Well then," he replied, "at the rate you have been going, working at it only at night and during the summer, you will be an old man before you finish. Why don't you come down to College Park full-time. I'll give you a laboratory instructor's job which pays eight hundred dollars per year, but gives you free tuition and free laboratory fees."

It was an offer I could not refuse and in the fall of 1939 I reported to Dr. White for work. I also stopped in to see President Curley Byrd who greeted me warmly, asked about Vic, and told me if I ever needed any help to call on him. I knew this was a rhetorical statement only, but it was still a comforting one, and one of the reasons why Dr. Byrd remained sort of a hero to me ever after.

Curley Was a Byrd

I FIRST became aware of Harry Clifton "Curley" Byrd when he took his University of Maryland football team to New Haven, Connecticut, and scored a decisive 15 to 0 upset victory over the Yale Bulldogs in 1926. Today it would excite no particular comment in Maryland or elsewhere if Maryland defeated Yale in football. The Maryland Terrapins usually rank among the top twenty college football teams in the nation while Yale is usually further down the list even though the Bulldogs win more than their share of Ivy League championships. But things were different in 1926 because the Bulldog was then a ferocious animal with a growl that frightened many opponents and a bite which could crack bones. Consequently, Yale expected to beat just about every team it played and certainly did not expect to be mauled by an upstart team from south of the Mason-Dixon line. In fact, not many of the small group of Maryland fans which accompanied Curley's team to New Haven expected the Terrapins to come home with a victory.

Wilson's column "On The Gridiron," which in those days appeared regularly in the *Baltimore Sun* during the football season, took note of this sensational victory by carrying the following brief poem at the top of the column.

When the boys are in a panic
Dreading foes that loom titanic,
Watch the man who grows satanic,
Shouts "absurd."
This gent loves to find 'em burly,

Before the Bridge

Brainy, brawny, sour, and surly.
You can't reckon without Curley
He's a Byrd.

Although I never met Curley, as everyone in Maryland called him, until Wilson introduced me to him in 1935, by which time his great victory over Yale had become ancient history, I already knew a great amount about him, mostly from reports given to me by Wilson and Vic. Wilson had been writing about Curley for many years and had high regard for his coaching ability. He told me that Curley was a brilliant and inventive coach of football with leadership qualities and intuitive good judgment which very few football coaches in the nation ever equalled. In fact, he told me that it was a truly remarkable thing that Maryland had two such coaches during the 1920s and 1930s. The other outstanding football strategist and psychologist in the state, Wilson said, was Dick Harlow who coached at Western Maryland College and scored some astonishing upsets of his own, working from a much smaller base than Curley had at College Park. Harlow's record was so remarkable, in fact, that in 1935 Harvard University lured him away from Western Maryland by making him both head coach of football and professor of oology at Harvard. That second title so amazed the sportswriters that they were still explaining, two years later, that oology was the study of birds' eggs and that Harlow had the finest collection of birds' eggs in North America.

Wilson admired Curley's mastery of the art and psychology of football, but he also admired his deftness as a politician even though this admiration was tinged with a touch of amusement and cynicism which was reflected in that last line of the poem above.

Vic's reaction to Curley lacked that trace of reservation which Wilson had about him. Vic played football under Curley and had worked in the business office of the University, which Curley once supervised in his capacity as assistant to President Pearson. To Vic, Curley was all hero. Even Curley's well-established reputation as a ladies' man, whether the ladies involved

Curley Was a Byrd

were coeds, pretty young female professors in the English Department, or matrons in various Maryland communities, did not distub Vic to the slightest degree. He called Curley a "noble stag" and treated any adverse comments in this direction as compliments.

The closest I ever heard Vic come to criticizing Curley was really not a criticism at all but a laughing recognition of the fact that Curley was after all quite human. Shortly after Vic came home from Europe and World War II, he stopped by College Park to see Curley who then had been president there for about ten years. Curley's secretary, as was her custom when old favorites came to see Curley, sent Vic into the inner office unannounced. There he found Curley reading a Bible.

"How are you, Curley?"

"Vic, I couldn't be better mentally and physically, but spiritually I need improvement. And so I'm reading the Bible."

Later, with his eyes dancing, Vic told me about this exchange and added: "I suspect that Curley was right on all three counts."

It should be noted here, although the comment won't be needed by all who knew him during his prime years, that Curley was not a born again Christian even though he was famous for the large collection of Bibles which he owned and read frequently. Curley was a student of philosophy and religion who accepted some of the ideas he encountered in these fields but rejected many others.

Harry Clifton Byrd was born in Crisfield, only about twenty miles, by water, from where I was born. The Somerset County where he grew up was quite similar to my own Dorchester County. Curley took great pride in his home territory. When he was in a position of influence as director of athletics and assistant to the president, he arranged to have the University of Maryland's athletic teams be given the nickname of Terrapins (later shortened to Terps), and the student newspaper to be named the *Diamondback*. Both of these names, of course, were in honor of Maryland's famous seafood delicacy, the diamondback terrapin, which flourished in the marshes around Crisfield.

Before the Bridge

After graduating from high school Curley obtained a broad and liberal education by attending four institutions of higher education—the Maryland Agricultural College, George Washington University, Western Maryland College, and Georgetown University. He played football at all four institutions, but obtained his only earned college degree, bachelor of arts, from the first of the four. In later years when his political influence was a statewide matter, Curley was fond of reminding any appropriate audience that he was an alumnus of all four and had thoroughly enjoyed his undergraduate days at each one of them. However, there was never any doubt about the fact that his most abiding loyalty was to the Maryland Agricultural College and to the University of Maryland in which the agricultural college was incorporated in 1920.

In 1912 Curley persuaded President Silvester of the Maryland Agricultural College to appoint him to the position of instructor in English and athletics. He remained at College Park for the next forty-two years while supervising, in various capacities, the development of one of the nation's great universities.

Just when Harry C. Byrd was first called Curley is not known, but the name probably was given to him during his high school years and he was known by it throughout his long association with the University of Maryland. It never ceased to be an appropriate nickname. Even when Curley was seventy and his once black hair had turned completely white he still had a thick mass of curls all over the top of his head. There was no trace of a bald spot, and his forehead was not appreciably higher than it had been in his undergraduate days.

Curley's college yearbook carried beneath his picture the statement that "The Devil hath power to assume a pleasing shape," and some of his foes saw fit to see a special significance in this statement by his undergraduate peers. However, no one, throughout his long career, ever disputed the fact that Curley was an extraordinarily handsome fellow with great personal magnetism.

Curley was President of the University of Maryland for almost two decades. His most spectacular achievements came

Dr. Harry Clifton "Curley" Byrd. Curley was a remarkable combination of athlete, coach, university president, philosopher, conservationist, student of the Bible, and above all a Byrd.

in the years 1940 to 1950, when the physical plant of the University quadrupled in size, and the student body increased by a factor of seven. Curley became known all over the nation as an educator who knew how to obtain funds from both public and private sources.

The two most widely read magazines in the nation during that period, *Saturday Evening Post* and *Collier's*, featured stories about him. The *Post's* story was entitled "Curley Byrd Catches the Worm," while the story in *Collier's* was called "Maryland's Busiest Byrd." Both called attention to his handsomeness as well as his great personal magnetism and executive ability.

In fact, Curley became known all over the world when the University of Maryland began to operate branches in such distant places as Heidelberg, Germany, Thule, Greenland, and Dhahran on the Persian Gulf, for the benefit of American soldiers who were then stationed all over the world. These branches were called University College, and in 1954 the enrollment in this one college totaled more than ten thousand students. Curley believed and occasionally said that he had accomplished what he set out to do when he became president in 1935—make the University of Maryland one of the great universities of the world.

Nevertheless, his administration, despite its many spectacular achievements, never lacked criticism and enemies. From the beginning many in academic circles, both outside and within the university itself, felt that Curley was not qualified to be head of an academic institution. They pointed out that his one earned degree, bachelor of arts, was from an agricultural college, and were not at all placated when Curley quickly picked up a dozen or so honorary doctorates and became "Dr. Byrd." In fact, Curley set what probably was a record when he received two honorary doctorates during a period of about an hour; he flew by helicopter from Dickinson College in Pennsylvania to Western Maryland College at Westminister in setting this record. His critics said this feat only demonstrated his academic insecurity.

Even in 1937, before the explosive growth period began in 1940, some of Curley's critics felt the University of Maryland

Curley Was a Byrd

was becoming too big for excellence in academic work. The *Baltimore Sun* was one of these critics.

The *Sun* had never been charmed by Curley's magnetic personality and in 1937 the editors persuaded H. L. Mencken to make a study of the university and report on it to the citizens of Maryland. Mencken had long been famous for devastating criticisms of all sorts of individuals and institutions and had written several essays about the "rolling mills" of education as he called all large universities. It is highly likely that at least some of the *Sun* editors hoped that Mencken would cut Curley and his fast growing institution to pieces.

But alas for Curley's foes, Mencken took a liking to Dr. Byrd and was not at all disturbed that he had only one earned degree. Degrees, or lack of them, meant nothing to Mencken; he had no earned degrees himself and had refused two dozen or so offers of honorary doctorates from various prestigious colleges and universities. Mencken had been offered so many honorary degrees that he finally put a stop to the offers by issuring a statement which said:

> No decent man would accept a degree he hadn't earned. Honorary degrees are for corporation presidents, bishops, real-estate agents, Presidents of the United States, and other such riff-raff.

In any event, Mencken liked what he saw at the University of Maryland and opened his series of articles about it by saying

> The University of Maryland, now a majestic stream of culture as wide as the Amazon, with thousands of tax-payers rowing for their lives across its glittering bosom, arose in the dark backward and abysm of time, as a series of trickling rills.

It was a typical Mencken sentence, sparkling with witty allusions and wild exaggerations, but having a solid core of truth at the heart of it. And all that followed showed that the Sage of Baltimore was more nearly in full agreement with

187

Curley than with his critics. Mencken closed his series by
calling Curley an efficient executive who should have even
greater responsibilities given to him. He recommended, perhaps with tongue in cheek, that all the other colleges and
universities in the state be combined with the University of
Maryland, thereby making it an even more majestic stream of
culture than it was in 1937—with Curley in charge of them all.

> The thing to do with a man of such talents is not to cuss
> him for doing his job so well; it is far wiser, so long as
> hanging him is unlawful, to give him a bigger and better
> one.

This review, combined with the spectacular nature of
Curley's own performance in providing new buildings, more
students, and outstanding faculty scholars to the campus at
College Park, quieted his critics for a while. But the criticism
slowly began to build again in volume and by the time Curley
concluded that he had finished the job he set out to do and
resigned so he could run for governor of Maryland, it was
louder than it had ever been before. In fact it was so loud that it
was a significant factor in Curley's defeat at the polls. After he
lost his bid to become governor of Maryland, Curley per-
formed one more great service for his state. As chairman of
the Tidewater Fisheries Commission, he was instrumental in
reviving the Chesapeake Bay oyster industry, nearly doubling
the number of bushels of oysters harvested annually. His most
spectacular success in this work came when he convinced the
legislature and Governor Tawes that the dredging up of millions of bushels of oyster shells buried under the mud of the
Chesapeake should be carried out. These shells were then
dumped along known oyster bars to provide a firm base for
the attachment of new young oysters.

In this program, Curley once again displayed the powers
of persuasion which had characterized him during his early
years at the University of Maryland. But the things I remember best about him are the occasions when I personally saw
these powers in action.

Curley Was a Byrd

After I was introduced to him in 1935, Curley always professed to know me whenever we met although I noticed that he was not quite sure, for the first year or two, what my name was unless I was accompanied by Wilson or Vic. When they were along, he always greeted me warmly and by my first name. This recognition by Curley of the importance of knowing first names is, of course, an old trick of all good politicians, but I saw Curley overdo it once.

I was in the drugstore in Glen Burnie one day in 1937 talking to Howard Pfund about Curley, who was scheduled to speak there that day, and Howard said he would like to meet him. The words had scarcely passed Howard's lips when in walked Curley. I grabbed Howard by the hand and rushed him over to where Curley was drinking a coke.

"Curley," I said, "do you know Howard Pfund? I'd like you to meet him."

What I said was stupidly worded because I knew Curley did not know Howard, but Curley never hesitated.

"Of course I know him," he said. "How are you, Howard?"

The other occasion when I met with Curley in Glen Burnie, he was more surefooted. Miss Motley, Principal of the Glen Burnie High School, asked me if I could arrange to have Curley speak to the graduating class that year, and I said I would try. When I called Curley on the phone, he took a minute to check his calendar and then accepted immediately. Miss Motley then wrote him a letter of thanks and confirmation and signed her name L. Tod Motley, according to her long established custom.

When graduation night arrived, I met Curley at the entrance to the school building. He immediately asked to meet the principal.

"I don't think I have ever met Mr. Motley," he said.

I told him that Mr. Motley was really Miss Louisa Tod Motley, and that her signature fooled him as it did so many others. Curley grinned.

"She is obviously a smart girl because she knows that men find it easier to advance into executive positions than women do. We need more like her at the university."

Before the Bridge

I took Curley up to the front of the auditorium where Miss Motley was and while the three of us were talking, a messenger arrived from the front door with an urgent problem for her. A Mr. Mahon, from Baltimore, was there to see his nephew graduate but had no ticket and there were none left to give him. Whereupon Mr. Mahon had told the ticket taker that he was "with Dr. Byrd," the speaker. Miss Motley showed that she was a forthright executive.

"Is he?"

"Mr. Mahon is a distinguished member of the state legislature. If your question is, did he come here with me, the answer is no. But is he with me? The answer is yes. He is always with me. Please give him a seat even if it has to be mine."

Mr. Mahon got a seat in a chair up front.

But the Curley I like best to remember was the Curley of 1941 when he was at the peak of his powers and abilities. That year Curley went before the legislature to defend his proposed budget for the university, and by 1941 even more taxpayers were rowing for their lives than Mencken had noticed in 1937. Consequently, Curley knew that since the legislature would be likely to question any item of expense in his proposed budget, he prepared diligently, prior to his appearance before the budget committee.

One item in the budget was for fifteen or twenty thousand dollars to fund a research program on diatomaceous earth deposits recently discovered in southern Maryland. This item caused one of Curley's foes to think he might have found a way of making the football coach, now turned university president, look foolish. The word diatomaceous was new to the legislator and he thought it might also be strange to an ex-football player, holding only honorary doctoral degrees.

"Just what is diatomaceous earth, Dr. Byrd? And why in the world should we spend taxpayer's money on it?"

Whereupon Curley launched into a dissertation on diatomaceous earth which astounded his audience. He described the tiny sea animals whose shells had gone into the formation of diatomaceous earth deposits. He gave its general chemical composition, told how the ancient Egyptians had used it with powdered iron oxide to make a rouge for Cleopatra, and explained its modern uses in water purification and chemical catalysis. He concluded by saying that while financial returns could never be guaranteed on any research program, this one had better than average prospects. He said that most diatomaceous earth used in the United States came as Kieselguhr imported from Germany and that source of supply might be cut off by developments from the war then in progress, while new sources in South Africa, Norway, and Australia were as untested as the recent discoveries in Maryland. His answer stopped all questioning about his budget which then was approved without comment by the committee.

I had long believed that Curley's critics underestimated him badly. He was far better educated than they realized because his program of self-education had been one which he continued throughout his life. His interest in Bibles and philosophers was a genuine and abiding one, and everything in Maryland interested him. Nevertheless, as much as I admired him and as deep and as wide as I knew his knowledge was, it puzzled me that he had, at his fingertips, so much information about one word in a two hundred-page budget report.

So one day in the summer of 1941 I mentioned my puzzlement to Vic when we went to see Charlie Keller and his New York Yankee teammates play Washington in baseball. Vic had stopped in to see Curley before he came over to pick me up at the chemistry building where I was then working. Vic was in a high humor, as he usually was after talking with Curley, and he grinned broadly when I told him how Curley had conquered the legislature earlier that year.

"Curley has always been too smart for those guys," he said, "but I wouldn't be surprised to learn that he had a confederate plant that question for him."

I told Vic that the question had come from a fellow who had long been one of Curley's foes in the legislature so that Vic's explanation was not likely to be the real answer. However, in thinking about it some more I have come to suspect that Curley really may have planted a spy in the camp of his enemies, and this spy somehow managed to bait the hook

Before the Bridge

which lodged so firmly in the throat of Curley's enemy that day.

After all, Curley really was a Byrd.

TWENTY

The Death of Humility

THE graduate students in chemistry at the University of Maryland in 1940 were divided into two classes: those Dr. Drake greeted by their first names and those who were on a sort of probation list and were hailed by their last names only. I was in the second category.

Nathan Lincoln Drake, head of the department of chemistry at College Park, was a Bostonian with an A so broad that he said "hahm" when he asked for a ham and cheese sandwich at Albrecht's drugstore where he ate lunch on rare occasions. He had graduated from Harvard with a bachelor's degree in 1920 and then went on there to earn a master's degree in 1921 and a doctorate in organic chemistry in 1922. As all full-fledged chemists were expected to do in those days, he went to Europe for further study and research, working with the famous chemist Ruzicka in Zurich, Switzerland. Still later he worked as an industrial chemist for three years before becoming professor of organic chemistry at College Park in 1928. With a Phi Beta Kappa key dangling from his watch chain he moved with great assurance in chemical and academic circles.

Dr. Drake and President Curley Byrd got along well, partly because Curley paid his scientific professors more than he paid those holding comparable positions in the liberal arts, and Drake was the most highly paid of the scientists. Curley had been forced to do this in order to lure Drake away from his job in industry. However, I suspect that another reason why they got along well was that both of them recognized exceptional competence when they saw it in others.

Dr. Drake was one of those who led the way when Dr. Byrd and the University of Maryland were attracting huge sums of money from the federal government for work on the national defense effort, prior to and during World War II. Among other honors, Dr. Drake received the Hillebrand Prize for his work on anti-malarial compounds when the Japanese cut off supplies of quinine.

While his activities as head of the department of chemistry were beginning to cut in on his time as professor of organic chemistry, he still served in that capacity in 1940, and I was lucky enough to have him as research advisor. But Dr. Drake fell completely outside the long established picture of a college professor of days gone by—the kindly, doddering, absent-minded old fellow with a heart of gold.

Dr. Drake was about as absentminded as an end on the football team who has just caught a pass behind the last defensive back and is racing for the goal line. Instead of doddering he was full of vinegar after five sets of tennis or an afternoon of glass blowing in the laboratory. He maintained a schedule of work and recreation which astonished his students and caused one of them to declare he was pursued by his own pack of Furies, which obviously were more unrelenting than Alecto, Megaera and Tisiphone, of Greek mythology. He was a sailor, an archer, a tennis player, and an organist who still averaged about twelve hours per day in the laboratories and lecture halls.

Despite his middle name of Lincoln, his motto was not "with malice toward none, with charity for all." He had some charitable moments, but his students all swore these never occurred when he was grading papers. His contempt for those who were lazy or stupid was so close to malice that he apparently saw no reason to correct anyone who assumed that it really was malice. He was the terror of premedical students who were required to pass organic chemistry to gain entrance into medical school, and he regularly flunked about half of them. One year a group of premedical students got up a petition against him and took it to President Byrd, claiming that Dr. Drake was unfair to medicine. Curley delivered the students a firm lecture on the obligation which the state had to make sure that its doctors were really prepared to minister to

Nathan Lincoln Drake. Professor of organic chemistry at the University of Maryland, head of the Department of Chemistry, and hero of the inquisition.

the sick, and he and Dr. Drake had a good laugh in private over this failed petition.

Homer Carhart, one of my associates in the graduate school, said that Drake had done more than even Hippocrates to raise the standards of medicine in Maryland. I remember standing near Dr. Drake one day while an assistant instructor was putting locks on the laboratory desks of all who had failed the first semester of organic chemistry that year, and I mentioned to him that the fatality rate seemed unusually high. He pulled deeply on his pipe, removed it from his mouth, grinned wickedly, and said: "Well, we aren't here to entertain them."

That was an understatement of huge dimensions because he was a slave driver of renown. In fact, his graduate students called him, behind his back, Simon Legree and later with wry affection changed that to Marse Simon.

But this ogre, this tiger who mauled so many premedical students was enormously helpful in the laboratory because he was as skillful with his hands as he was fertile in ideas as to how a chemical research problem should be pursued. He was a good glass blower and thoroughly enjoyed a session with an acetylene torch or a welding iron.

Also, he could be almost as charming as his lovely wife—when it suited him—and it always suited him to behave in his most charming manner when he invited the slaves to his house for a social gathering and dinner after the cotton had been picked and baled. Unfortunately, only members of the first name club were invited to his home for a jubilee, and throughout the academic year of 1939-40 I thought I would never make it.

Despite the fact that I had completed one research project under his direction and had received a master's degree, Dr. Drake clearly still was uncertain about how he should treat me. Other members of the first name club such as Joe Lann, Bill Stanton, Jack Wolf, and Homer Carhart were very friendly to me, but I was still Wingate to Marse Simon until one hot Sunday night in August, 1940.

I was all alone at about midnight that day working on the "active hydrogen machine" in the third floor research labora-

The Death of Humility

tory when Dr. Drake suddenly walked in. He paused briefly behind me, looked over my shoulder at the complicated glass apparatus which he and Harry Anspon had built, and then said, more softly than was usually the case when he spoke to me: "What progress, Phil?"

He did not wait for an answer but strode quickly into his office near the rear of the laboratory and just as quickly came back out and was gone. His failure to wait for an answer was not important because I had no real progress to report. But that last word was enormously important, and I even began to wonder if I had imagined it.

Had I really been inducted into the first name club at midnight? Dr. Drake removed all doubt about my new status the very next day when he sat in his office and roared out for all to hear: "Phil, come in here. I want to talk to you."

I went in with great rejoicing, and also went to the next sliced ham and turkey dinner which he held at his house for the first name club. There I confirmed what had been told to me by others: Mrs. Drake really did make the world's best apple pie.

And when the next jubilee after that one was scheduled for January, 1941, I drove home to Dorchester County and came back with a bushel of oysters taken from the deep cold waters of the Chesapeake between Crocheron and Crisfield. These oysters were not quite as salty as Chincoteagues or Lynnhavens but they were even fatter and tastier because they had fed, all their lives, on the rich soup coming out of the great marshes of Dorchester and Somerset Counties.

I was the official shucker that night and gained an undeserved reputation as an expert at opening oysters—simply because in the kingdoms of the blind even a one-eyed man is likely to become emperor. Many of the others present that night probably would have thought that a hammer, not a knife, was the proper tool for opening oysters. Dr. Drake was intrigued by my shucking technique and asked why I always put the cupped side of the oyster down before trying to insert the knife blade. When I explained that this made it possible to locate the thinnest part of the shell lip, he grinned and said:

Before the Bridge

"I'll have another one."

He liked people who were skillful with their hands, and my exploits with the oyster knife, plus the tastiness of the end product, probably removed any lingering doubts he may have had about the wisdom of admitting me to the first name club. Harry Anspon and Jack Wolf were particular favorites of his because they were expert glass blowers.

Al Whiton had never eaten an oyster on the half shell before that night, but after he gingerly downed one, he became my best customer and ate two dozen more. I had been tempted to propose partly freezing some oysters in the freezer section of Mrs. Drake's refrigerator, to improve their taste, but decided that she might object to putting oysters in their shells in with her other foods, so the first name club missed out on this taste refinement. It may have been a good thing that they did because Al Whiton might then have eaten another two dozen.

A few years ago I wrote an article for the university magazine, *Maryland,* and in it said that Dr. Drake's graduate students thought he was the best chemist in the country and that he concurred in that opinion. Dr. Drake had died a few years earlier when he suffered a heart attack while playing golf, a new sport for him, but his daughter, Ruth Drake Davis, noticed the piece and took exception to the second half of that claim. She wrote me that she knew her father thought he was a very good chemist but "surely didn't think he was the best."

My original statement in the piece for *Maryland* was made without much thought but after full consideration I still think it was right in both parts. He was the best chemist in the country, and he was too smart not to know it. I thought so then and have not changed my mind after forty years of mingling with chemists of all ranks and abilities, from toilers at the bench to Nobel laureates and other dignitaries among the nobility and gentry of chemistry.

One of the things which made Dr. Drake such a great scientist was his irreverent attitude. He accepted no man's opinions or theories as gospel—not even his own, although it seemed at times that he might make an exception there. Everything, in his opinion, was subject to the rigorous test of the laboratory. If he had lived in the time of Aristotle and Plato, he probably would have laughed the ancient Greeks out of their imaginative ideas about chemistry a couple of thousand years before Lavoisier and Dalton did it by running some experiments.

Dr. Drake laughed heartily when I gave a seminar report, one time, on the fierce argument then going on between Linus Pauling and Dorothy Wrinch on the structure of protein molecules. This was before Carothers had shown that long chain molecules could easily exist, and Dr. Pauling and Dr. Wrinch were debating about whether proteins were large rings or just folded chains.

"They both sound too vehement," he said, "for the little bit they know about the subject, but if I had to guess, I'd say Pauling is closer to being right."

Dr. Pauling is now known all over the world for his two Nobel Prizes and his belief that vitamin C may cure all sorts of things from common colds to cancer. If Dr. Drake were still around, I suspect he might say again that Dr. Pauling seems too vehement for what he knows.

While Dr. Drake had high confidence in his own opinions he respected those who challenged him and spoke back—if their position was solidly based. One day he brought a large packet of letters and open envelopes which had been prepared by his hard working secretary, Lucy Lynham, and threw them on the desk of Janet Scott, an undergraduate liberal arts student who was earning some pocket money as a part-time secretary in the chemistry department.

"Here, Miss Scott, lick these, stamp them, and put them in the mail."

Miss Scott was not a chemistry student, she didn't absolutely have to have the money she was earning, and she didn't like the peremptory tone of the order.

"Here, Dr. Drake," she said, pushing the envelopes away from her, "lick them yourself."

He looked at her in stunned silence for a second, picked up the letters without a word, and carried them away. Whether he licked them himself as directed by the sassy Miss Scott or took them back to the overworked Miss Lynham I never learned, but Miss Scott kept her job and was henceforth treated with both courtesy and friendliness by Dr. Drake.

The steroid chemicals in those days were just beginning to be recognized for their great importance in biological processes, and Dr. Drake became an enthusiast on the subject. He taught a course on the chemistry of steroids and assigned Gordon Dittmar the research project of learning as much as he could about the structure of the steroid found in the bark of the cork tree. Then he gave me the job of learning how to insert an angular methyl group into the naphthalene molecule so that it could be used as a building block for all the steroid chemicals which contained this peculiar configuration.

While I was working on this project, Vic came to see me one day and asked what I was doing. I told him I was trying to make an intermediate for steroid chemicals.

"What are they?"

"Some of them are important as sex hormones and surprisingly they are chemically the same whether they are found in human beings or in other animals. I'm glad I'm working on an intermediate chemical for the steroids because other people working on sex hormones have to extract them from the urine of horses, cows, or other animals."

Vic almost exploded with laughter.

"Well, I'll be damned. I gave a ride to a boy who was hitchhiking from Easton to Cambridge last week, and he told me he had a job working at a horse farm near Easton but he was going to quit because the farmer was crazy. He said the farmer had him spending most of his time collecting horse urine which the farmer said he shipped to some chemists in Philadelphia. I thought the boy was giving me a bunch of bull, but maybe he wasn't."

I never was able to develop a procedure for putting angular methyl groups in a naphthalene molecule and, so far as I know, no one else ever did either. Anyway, I gave up on this project after several months, and Dr. Drake then suggested

The Death of Humility

that I study the oxidation of pyrethrosin for my major research study.

Pyrethrosin was one of the other natural products which he and some of his students had been studying for several years without learning how to write its structural formula. It was an inert ingredient in the pyrethrin powders which were much in demand as an insecticide then. The pyrethrins were used in Black Flag and other products used to kill house flies.

The University of Maryland, in those days, had a number of requirements for a Ph.D. degree in chemistry and among them were: (1) passing a series of examinations called prelims, (2) completing an original piece of research to "add to the existing body of chemical knowledge" to be written and accepted as a thesis, and finally (3) passing an oral examination by a faculty committee.

The first two were genuine obstacle tests which, much too often for the mental comfort of the graduate students, resulted in a failure which washed them right out of the graduate school. Unlike baseball, two strikes were out. When a candidate failed twice to pass the prelims, he was finished. And a continuing nightmare for those doing research projects was that after the project had been completed, but before it was written up and accepted as a thesis, someone else might publish essentially the same information in a chemical journal. Then, of course, it would not add anything to the existing body of chemical knowledge, and so the poor student would have to begin all over again.

The third requirement was different. No one had ever failed the oral examination although one candidate for a Ph.D. degree had lost his voice halfway through the examination, and had to be granted a recess until he recovered it. Some months after I joined the first name club, Dr. Drake told me that the oral exam was simply "a final opportunity for the faculty to teach the candidate a proper sense of humility." It was well suited to that purpose because the poor candidate, all alone, was required to "defend his thesis" before a group of five or six professors who were free to attack him from any direction which suited their whims.

Despite the fact that I ran out of money entirely late in 1941 and had to borrow from Evelyn, my final year at College Park was a vintage one. The Guild Theatre in Baltimore presented a series of Gilbert and Sullivan shows for fifty cents a ticket and, using my borrowed money, I took a blue-eyed blond graduate of Western Maryland College to see all of them. I read H. L. Mencken's latest book, *Happy Days,* and found it to be the most delightful thing the Sage of Baltimore had written up to that time. In addition Jack Faber and Al Heagy gave me the job of refereeing the freshman lacrosse games in the spring of 1942 and paid me forty dollars for this job which I would gladly have done for nothing.

Finally, everything began to fall into place on my research project. While nothing had worked for me on the angular methyl venture, everything began to work as planned on pyrethrosin.

I knew that what I was doing would have about the same impact on the broad stream of chemical knowledge that a single snowflake falling in the Susquehanna River at Havre de Grace would have on the temperature of the Chesapeake Bay at Norfolk a week later. Nevertheless, the work was fascinating when the pieces began to fall into place.

I found, for example, that the fifth atom in pyrethrosin was part of a secondary alcohol! This startling piece of information will create no more headlines today than it did then, but when I oxidized the alcohol to a ketone and made a dinitro phenyl hydrazone of the ketone, the red crystals which I then isolated were as exciting to me as Halley's Comet had been to Mark Twain. Soon I had synthesized a dozen or so new compounds made from pyrethrosin and never before seen by anyone. Dr. Drake and I agreed that I then had enough new chemical knowledge for a thesis and that I should write it up.

When I bragged to Evelyn about my new compounds she asked me why I had chosen the inert ingredient of pyrethrin powder for my research work. Why not the active ingredient? I gave her a lame answer about never knowing when a piece of chemical information might prove to be important in the

The Death of Humility

future. I even mentioned the fact that the new wonder drugs, the sulfanilamides, had stood idle for a quarter of a century after they had first been synthesized in Germany.

However, the truth of the matter was: (1) Dr. Drake had suggested my topic, and (2) the active ingredient had already been thoroughly studied, and I was required to do something original.

It did not really matter to me whether my new compounds were active or inactive, useful or useless. I had the material for a thesis, I had a firm offer of a job from the Du Pont Company as soon as I received a Ph.D. degree, and all that stood between me and that degree was the oral examination.

Although I reminded myself that Dr. Drake himself had told me that the oral examination was essentially a formality, designed to give the faculty one last chance to teach me humility, nevertheless my mouth was dry and the palms of my hands were wet when I went in to face the inquisitors. Dr. Drake was presiding and he started out by asking Dr. Malcolm Haring, professor of physical chemistry, if he had any questions about my thesis. Dr. Haring was a kindly fellow whom the graduate students called Uncle Mac, and he asked a few simple questions that a freshman could have answered. So I quickly realized that Uncle Mac was simply trying to make me feel at ease. That helped.

Next came Dr. Charles E. White, professor of inorganic chemistry and the man who had given me the job which permitted me to attend the University of Maryland. He also treated me in a kindly fashion and by the time he finished with me I was off and running.

In fact, everything went amazingly well until it was Dr. Peter Oesper's turn to question me. He was a brilliant young physical chemist only recently graduated from Princeton.

"Why did you work on the inactive ingredient?" he asked. "Why didn't you work on something useful?"

I replied that if we learned the structure of pyrethrosin, the inert ingredient, we might rather simply convert it into the active ingredient, thereby making pyrethrum flowers more effective as an insecticide. I also gave him the bit about never knowing what new piece of scientific knowledge might one day be very important to the human race. I even hinted that the oxime of dehydropyrethrosin, which I had invented, might some day cure cancer or the common cold.

Dr. Oesper was not impressed, and I sensed he had heard that line before. He kept on badgering me with several other questions, all suggesting that I had wasted my research time. I answered these questions as best I could, always avoiding the real answer which was, of course, that Dr. Drake had suggested the project. During these answers I did, however, glance occasionally at Dr. Drake and saw that he was becoming impatient with Dr. Oesper's line of questioning.

It is one thing for a bright, young associate professor to teach humility to a candidate before the committee, and quite another for him to try to teach it, even unknowingly, to a Harvard Phi Beta Kappa, who also happens to be the young professor's boss once removed.

Suddenly Dr. Drake broke in on a question and said rather abruptly to Dr. Haring: "Malcom, do you have any further questions?"

"No," replied Uncle Mac, and Dr. Drake then turned toward Dr. White. But Dr. Oesper stepped back in before Dr. White had a chance to speak.

"I'd like to pursue the question of the choice of the research project a little further," he said.

I saw Dr. Drake's long jaw harden and the sight of it made me bold. I was on the winning side and I knew it.

"You have already pursued it past me, Dr. Oesper," I said.

Dr. Drake threw back his head and roared with laughter while his feet hit the floor with a sound of finality.

"The examination is concluded," he said, and everyone, Dr. Oesper in particular, knew that it was. Then when Dr. Drake reached across his desk to shake my hand and congratulate me, humility, which had been gasping for breath for a minute or so, died quite suddenly.